Instructor's Manual with Test Bank for
Jaccard and Becker's

Statistics for the Behavioral Sciences

FOURTH EDITION

JAMES JACCARD
University of Albany, State University of New York

WADSWORTH

THOMSON LEARNING

Australia • Canada • Mexico • Singapore • Spain • United Kingdom • United States

COPYRIGHT © 2002 Wadsworth Group.
Wadsworth is an imprint of the Wadsworth Group, a division of Thomson Learning, Inc. Thomson Learning™ is a trademark used herein under license.

For more information about this or any other Wadsworth product, contact:
WADSWORTH
511 Forest Lodge Road
Pacific Grove, CA 93950 USA
www.wadsworth.com
1-800-423-0563 (Thomson Learning Academic Resource Center)

All rights reserved. Instructors of classes using Jaccard and Becker's *Statistics for the Behavioral Sciences, Fourth Edition* as a textbook may reproduce material from this publication for classroom use. Otherwise, no part of this work covered by the copyright hereon may be reproduced or used in any form or by any means—graphic, electronic, or mechanical, including photocopying, recording, taping, Web distribution, or information storage and retrieval systems—without the written permission of the publisher.

For permission to use material from this work, contact us by
www.thomsonrights.com
fax: 1-800-730-2215
phone: 1-800-730-2214

Printed in the United States of America

10   9   8   7   6   5   4   3   2   1

ISBN: 0-534-56927-7

Contents

Preface

Chapter 1	Introduction and Mathematical Preliminaries / 1
Chapter 2	Frequency and Probability Distributions / 10
Chapter 3	Measures of Central Tendency and Variability / 22
Chapter 4	Percentiles, Percentile Ranks, Standard Scores, and the Normal Distribution / 32
Chapter 5	Pearson Correlation and Regression: Descriptive Aspects / 43
Chapter 6	Probability / 53
Chapter 7	Estimation and Sampling Distributions / 65
Chapter 8	Hypothesis Testing: Inferences About a Single Mean / 75
Chapter 9	Research Design and Statistical Preliminaries for Analyzing Bivariate Relationship / 86
Chapter 10	Independent Groups t Test / 96
Chapter 11	Correlated Groups t Test / 111
Chapter 12	One-Way Between-Subjects Analysis of Variance / 124
Chapter 13	One-Way Repeated Measures Analysis of Variance / 139
Chapter 14	Pearson Correlation and Regression: Inferential Aspects / 151
Chapter 15	Chi Square Test / 164

Chapter 16 Nonparametric Statistical Tests / 176

Chapter 17 Two Way Between-Subjects Analysis of Variance / 186

Chapter 18 Overview and Extension / 205

Preface

This manual is designed to assist you in the preparation of materials for class. Each chapter corresponds to a chapter in the textbook. The same basic structure is used in each chapter. First, I provide some general comments about my experiences over the years in teaching the content of a given chapter. This section highlights areas that I have found students to have a particularly hard time with. Second, I present examples that can be used to illustrate numerical calculations in class. Instructors typically do not want to lecture from the same examples that are used in the textbook. This section is designed to give you other examples that can be used. For the early chapters, I tend to select examples from the social sciences in the broadest sense of the discipline. I have found it useful to illustrate descriptive statistics with variables that have meaningful metrics in their own rights (e.g., age, dollars, time) rather than arbitrary metrics that are characteristic of so many psychological constructs (e.g., self esteem). Students can relate to the former better than the latter in the context of descriptive statistics. However, the arbitrary metrics are much easier for the student to interpret in the context of comparing means between groups or computing correlations, so I shift to more social-psychological constructs in later chapters. Third, I provide answers to selected exercises in the textbook. About half of the problems that we give in the textbook do not provide the answers to the students, so that you can assign them for graded homework. I give you the answers here. However, I only provide answers to problems that involve calculations or where an answer is not obvious. For example, I do not provide answers for questions that ask for definitions or ask the student to explain things in words (I assume that you already know these answers). Rather, my goal is to spare you the tedium of working out the correct answers to problems that involve more extensive calculations. Fourth, I provide a test bank that can be used for exams.

Many of the test questions were taken from the manual for the second edition written by Doug Mandra. However, several of them have been edited. James Cranford also contributed a number of questions for this manual. I extend my sincere gratitude to them.

Chapter 1: Introduction and Mathematical Preliminaries

Comments to Instructors

Many students start a statistics course very apprehensive about it. Fortunately, the material in this chapter is easy enough that it helps build confidence in students as they see that they can master it. In my experience, students have the hardest time with the material on measurement. I spend extra class time on this concept, going over many examples with them. I describe experiments to the students and then ask them to identify the independent and dependent variables and identify if each is qualitative or quantitative. I also ask them to indicate what level of measurement probably characterizes the measures and why. I draw my examples from the many experiments described in the Exercise sections of later chapters.

I stress to my students that statistics is like a foreign language. You can not "cram" for it the night before an exam. They will be learning a new "vocabulary" and they must study it every night and become fluent with it. Otherwise they will be lost.

Examples for Class

To illustrate summation notation, you can use scores for 5 individuals who work in a small business. Define X as the number of days that an individual missed work in the past 6 months and Y as the amount of money the person gets paid for each day of work. Place the example for your students in the context of an organizational psychologist who studies absenteeism. The sum of X is the total number of missed days across the 5 workers. The multiplication of X times Y reflects the total amount of wages that an individual lost. The sum of XY is the total lost wages across individuals. It is difficult to identify a single example in which all of the different summation operations are conceptually meaningful (e.g., ΣX^2; $c\Sigma X^2$). I usually tell my students that some of the operations we perform on scores are not conceptually meaningful in their own right, but rather are used as intermediate steps towards the calculation of statistical indices (discussed in later chapters) that are meaningful. I then proceed to illustrate these "intermediate" expressions with the worker example presented above. This permits me to illustrate all of the different summation notations in a way students can relate to.

Answers to Selected Exercises

18. a. 12/52 = .23   c. 6/36 = .17
     b. 2/6 = .33   d. 12/52 = .23

20. a. 37   e. 128   i. 227   m. 1369
     b. 30   f. 4.625   j. 154   n. 900
     c. 15   g. 3.75   k. 77   o. 12
     d. 15   h. 1110   l. 66   p. 5

24. a. 4.89 e. 6.24   i. 1.00   m. 2.00
     b. 8.97 f. 2.62   j. 3.67   n. 2.00
     c. 1.42 g. 6.32   k. 12.25
     d. 4.14 h. .40   l. 9.72

26. Calculations for original scores:
     a. 24.74   b. 4.95   c. 612.28   d. 123.38

     Calculations for rounded scores:
     a. 24.72   b. 4.94   c. 611.08   d. 123.14

30. c

Test Questions

1. A statement proposing that something is true about a given phenomenon is called a ____.
   a. truism
   b. study
   *c. hypothesis
   d. systematic observation

2. The number of hours per week that someone watches violent television programs is an example of a(n):
   *a. variable
   b. constant
   c. level
   d. hypothesis

3. A phenomenon that takes on different values is termed ____.
   a. an error
   b. a constant
   *c. a variable
   d. none of the above

4. In a study of the effects of exercise on health, the independent variable is ____ and the dependent variable is ____.
   a. constant; variable
   b. variable; constant
   c. health; exercise
   *d. exercise; health

5. If one is studying intelligence as a consequence of differing child-rearing practices, then the measure of intelligence is called ____.
   a. an independent variable
   *b. a dependent variable
   c. a constant
   d. none of the above

6. If you were interested in studying the effects of varying preparatory instructions on the perception of pain during an injection, the instructions would be a(n) ____ variable and the amount of perceived pain would be a(n) ____ variable.
   *a. independent; dependent
   b. dependent; dependent
   c. secondary; independent
   d. independent; independent

3

7. Studies concerned with the effectiveness of subliminal perception have looked at changes in product desirability as a function of messages presented at sub-threshold levels of stimulation. In those studies, the measure of desirability is called the _____ variable.
a. control
b. independent
*c. dependent
d. qualitative

8. The process of translating empirical relationships between objects into numerical relationships is referred to as _____.
a. probability
b. randomization
*c. measurement
d. inferential statistics

9. When the categories of a variable can be ordered on some continuum or dimension, that variable is said to be measured on at least a(n) _____ level.
a. nominal
*b. ordinal
c. interval
d. ratio

10. _____ measures have the property that numerically equal distances on the scale represent equal distances on the dimension being measured.
a. nominal
b. ordinal
*c. interval
d. none of the above

11. An investigator studying race classified people into three racial categories--black, white, and Hispanic. This is an example of a(n) _____ variable.
*a. nominal
b. ordinal
c. interval
d. ratio

12. Variables measured on ordinal, interval, or ratio levels are known as _____ variables, while variables measured on a nominal level are called _____ variables.
*a. quantitative; qualitative
b. qualitative; quantitative
c. independent; dependent
d. random; systematic

13. Which of the following levels of measurement involves variables that are not qualitative?
a. ratio
b. interval
*c. nominal
d. ordinal

14. If three people are described to you as either short, average, or tall, then the level of measurement would be ____.
a. nominal
*b. ordinal
c. interval
d. ratio

15. A clinical psychologist studying the effects of different therapies categorizes patients according to whether they are or are not in therapy. In this case, therapy is a:
a. quantitative variable
b. measurement variable
*c. qualitative variable
d. random variable

16. A measure has as its referent:
a. an individual on whom the measure is taken
b. a time at which the measure is taken
c. a setting in which the measure is taken
*d. all of the above

17. The determination of whether a variable is measured on a(n) ____ level is usually a straightforward matter in the behavioral sciences.
*a. nominal
b. ordinal
c. interval
d. ratio

18. Variables that can assume only a finite number of values or that have a finite number of values that can occur between any two points are called ____ variables.
a. ordinal
*b. discrete
c. continuous
d. none of the above

19. A ____ variable can theoretically include an infinite number of values between any two points.
a. nominal
b. discrete
*c. continuous
d. none of the above

20. An example of a continuous variable is:
a. intelligence
b. reaction time
*c. both a and b
d. neither a nor b

21. The number of grains of sand in a sand box has ____ properties.
a. continuous
*b. discrete
c. ordinal
d. nominal

22. ____variables can assume only a finite number of values between any two points; ____ variables theoretically can assume an infinite number of values between any two points.
*a. Discrete; continuous
b. Continuous; discrete
c. Discrete; qualitative
d. Quantitative; continuous

23. The real limits of the number 20 are:
*a. 19.5 to 20.5
b. 19 to 21
c. 19.05 to 20.05
d. 19.025 to 20.075

24. The real limits of 1.672 are ____.
a. 1.672 and 1.6725
*b. 1.6715 and 1.6725
c. 1.67 and 1.68
d. 1.671 and 1.673

25. 6.39489 rounded to three decimal places is equal to ____.
a. 6.390   b. 6.394   * c. 6.395   d. 6.400

26. A ____ is the aggregate of all cases to which one wishes to generalize statements.
a. sample
b. total sample
c. parameter
*d. population

27. A sample is simply a(n):
a. aggregate of all cases
b. random population
*c. subset of the population
d. statistic

28. On the basis of observing the ____, the researcher makes generalizations to the ____.
a. population; sample
*b. sample; population
c. subjects; variables
d. statistics; sample

29. One procedure for approximating representative samples is through:
*a. random sampling
b. nonrandom sampling
c. systematic studies
d. convenience sampling

30. The essential characteristic of random sampling is that every member of the population:
a. is selected for the study
b. is systematically selected
*c. has an equal chance of being selected
d. is excluded on random criteria

31. The use of random sampling procedures:
a. guarantees that a sample will be representative of the population
b. does not guarantee that a sample will be representative of the population
c. will sometimes yield nonrepresentative samples
*d. both b and c are correct

32. Parameters are statistical indices based on data from:
a. a sample
b. a random sample
*c. a population
d. populations or samples

33. _____ involves the use of numerical indices to describe either a population or a sample.
*a. descriptive statistics
b. inferential statistics
c. parametric statistics
d. all of the above

34. Taking measurements on a sample and then, from the observations, inferring something about a population is known as ____:
a. random sampling
*b. inferential statistics
c. descriptive statistics
d. inferential parametrics

35. Numerical indices derived from population data are ____; numerical indices derived from sample data are ____.
a. parameters; parameters
b. statistics; statistics
c. statistics; parameters
*d. parameters; statistics

36. Numerical indices based on data from entire populations are called ____.
a. statistics
*b. parameters
c. inferences
d. qualitative values

37. A given probability must always range from:
*a. 0 to 1.00
b. 0 to 100.00
c. -1.0 to +1.0
d. none of the above

38. The probability of observing a head on the sixth toss after flipping a coin 5 times and observing five tails is ____.
a. 1/6
*b. 0.50
c. 1.00
d. 6 x 0.5

39. The probability of observing both an even and an odd number when rolling a 6-sided die is ____.
a. 1.00
b. .50
*c. 0
d. approximately .25

40. Calculate $\sum X$ and $\sum X^2$ for the following data set: 1,3,3,5.
a. 12; 144
b. 4; 62
*c. 12; 44
d. 62; 144

41. Given the scores 1, 1, 2, 2, 3, 3, 4, what is the value of the following summation notation?

$$\sum_{i=2}^{4} X$$

a. 15   b. 9   c. 10   *d. 5

42. If c is a constant having a value of five, then $\sum(X - c)^2$ for the scores 4, 6, and 10 would be ____.
*a. 27   b. 14   c. $(20 - 2)^2$ d. $(14 - 2)$

Given the following data for X and Y variables, calculate the expressions in Questions 43-45

Case	X	Y
1	1	-1
2	3	0
3	9	2

43. ΣXY
a. 13   *b. 17   c. 22   d. 39

44. $\Sigma X + \Sigma Y$
a. -11   c. 16
b. 13   *d. 14

45. $\Sigma(X + Y)$
a. 49   b. 9   *c. 14   d. 29

Chapter 2: Frequency and Probability Distributions

Comments to Instructors

The material in this chapter is straightforward and also helps to build student confidence in their ability to master statistics as they successfully learn and apply its contents. I have found that students sometimes make errors when constructing frequency histograms and polygons. There is a tendency to mistakenly put the frequencies on the abscissa and the scores of the independent variable on the ordinate, when the reverse should be done. Students are sometimes confused because frequency information *is* put on the abscissa for stem and leaf plots.

Examples for Class

To illustrate a frequency distribution, I find it best to use a small number of raw scores and then to construct a frequency table from these (much like what is done with the Hyperactivity example in the main text). One example you can use focuses on friendship patterns in which a group of 12 college students is asked to indicate the number of close friends that they have. Here is frequency data that you could use:

Number of friends	f	rf	cf	crf
5	1	.083	12	1.000
4	2	.167	11	.917
3	4	.333	9	.750
2	3	.250	5	.417
1	2	.167	2	.167

These data can also be used to effectively demonstrate frequency histograms and polygons.

Another strategy is to use an example based on data that are collected directly from the class, if the class is not too large. For example, you might ask each student what their age is (e.g., raise your hand if you are 18; if you are 19) and count the number of students who fall into each age group. Then construct a frequency distribution from this.

To illustrate the construction of grouped frequency data, you can use a study that characterizes the age of women who obtain abortions at a hospital. You can position these data for students in the context of a counseling psychologist who works at the clinic and who wants to get a sense for the age range of clients he or she will be seeing. A total of 200 women are interviewed. Start with five groups. The lowest age was 15 and the highest age was 44. This yields an interval of (42-15)/5 = 5.4, which we round to 5. The beginning score is 15, yielding the following groups:

Age	f	rf	cf	crf
40-44	2	.01	200	1.00
35-39	12	.06	198	.99
30-34	24	.12	186	.93
25-29	42	.21	162	.81
20-24	66	.33	120	.60
15-19	54	.27	54	.27

The relative frequencies of the ages map onto the results of a national study in the United States in the year 1987. These data can also be used to construct a grouped frequency histogram.

To illustrate a frequency distribution for a qualitative variable, you can use the following data reported by the FBI in 1991. The variable is the type of crime committed by a child under the age of 10, based on reports from police departments. For students, you can place the data in the context of a forensic psychologist who is studying criminal behavior in children. There are eight categories or levels of the variable. Out of a total of 17,772 recorded crimes by children under 10 years of age, the frequencies of each type are:

	f	rf	%
Murder	6	.0003	.03
Forcible Rape	81	.0046	.46
Robbery	238	.0134	1.34
Motor Vehicle Theft	253	.0142	1.42
Aggravated Assault	1,068	.0601	6.01
Arson	1,068	.0601	6.01
Burglary	3,395	.1910	19.10
Larceny-Theft	11,663	.6563	65.63

I personally find some of these statistics to be rather sobering (e.g., there were over 1,000 instances of aggravated assault by children under the age of 10).

To illustrate a bar graph, I use the following data from a sample of 1,000 high school seniors in the U.S. about whether they have ever used marijuana. Position these data for students in the context of a developmental psychologist studying drug use among adolescents:

	f
Used	326
Not Used	674

I construct the Y axis in units of 100, beginning at zero and ending at 700. The percentage of marijuana users in these data map onto the percentage of users observed in national studies for 1992.

For a line plot or frequency histogram with two groups, I graph the above data as one "group" and then I also plot data for a comparable sample of 1,000 high school seniors for the year 1980:

	f
Used	595
Not Used	405

The plots show how the use of marijuana has decreased rather dramatically from 1980 to 1992.

To illustrate a stem and leaf plot, I use a small number of scores from assessments of the number of hours that a group of 15 teens estimate they watch television each week. Place these data for students in the context of a school psychologist studying homework and leisure patterns of students.

5, 8, 10, 10, 12, 18, 20, 22, 22, 25, 27, 30, 32

Answers to Selected Exercises

5. 4 days = .100
    4 or more days = .900
    More than 4 days = .800

17.

Score	f	rf	cf	crf	%
120-129	5	.10	50	1.00	10
110-119	10	.20	45	.90	20
100-109	20	.40	35	.70	40
90-99	10	.20	15	.30	20
80-89	5	.10	5	.10	10

23. 129 - 80 = 49   49/10 = 4.9   Interval size is 5. Lowest interval is 80-84.

24.

Response Category	f	rf	%
Married	30	.60	60
Divorced	5	.10	10
Widowed	5	.10	10
Single	10	.20	20

37. c

Test Questions

1. A useful tool for summarizing a large set of data is a ____:
a. qualitative distribution
*b. frequency distribution
c. descriptive distribution
d. all of the above

2. A frequency distribution is a table that lists ____ on a variable and shows the number of individuals who obtained each ____.
*a. scores; value
b. classes; frequencies
c. frequencies; class
d. scores; frequency

3. A table that lists scores on a variable and shows the number of occurrences of each score is called a ____ distribution.
a. probability
*b. frequency
c. normal
d. density

4. If the scores of a class at midterm are 70, 70, 70, 80, 80, 90, 92, and 92, what is the relative frequency of the score 80?
a. 2
*b. .25
c. .125
d. 5/8

5. A relative frequency is:
a. the proportion of times that a score occurred
b. the number of scores of a given value divided by the total number of scores
c. usually a more informative statistic than an absolute frequency
*d. all of the above

6. The relative frequencies in a distribution will always sum to:
*a. 1.00
b. 100.00
c. relative frequencies can not be summed
d. none of the above

7. When a relative frequency is multiplied by 100, it reflects the ____ of times the score occurred.
a. proportion
*b. percentage
c. absolute frequency
d. cumulative frequency

8. The number of times that a score occurs divided by the total number of scores is termed a(n)_____.
*a. relative frequency
b. cumulative frequency
c. probability density
d. average distribution

9. Given the scores 50, 50, 60, 70, 80, 90, 92, 92, what is the cumulative relative frequency for a score of 90?
a. .125   b. .83   c. .25   *d. .75

10. For any given score, the cumulative frequency is the frequency associated with that score plus the sum of:
a. all frequencies
b. all frequencies above that score
*c. all frequencies below that score
d. all frequencies except for that score

11. When we are concerned with a continuous variable, such as the degree of hyperactivity, frequencies and relative frequencies should be thought of in terms of the _____ of the scores.
a. proportions   *c. real limits
b. percentages   d. a and b

12. Guidelines for grouping scores suggest you use _____ groups.
a. the fewest number of   *c. between 5 and 15
b. between 0 and 5   d. over 20

13. If the lowest score in a distribution is 47 and the highest score is 99 and you used six groups, what is the appropriate interval size?
a. 5   b. 2   *c. 10   d. 10.4

14. If the range of scores in a distribution were equal to 48 and you placed the scores within ten groups, what interval size should be used?
a. 4.8   *b. 5.0   c. 10   d. 4.0

15. Suppose you were given 102 scores which ranged from 0 to 45 and you were asked to create a grouped frequency distribution using 15 intervals. What would be the most appropriate starting value?
*a. 0   b. 15   c. 3   d. 7

16. As a rule of thumb, the use of _____ groups in a grouped frequency distribution tends to strike the appropriate balance between imprecision and incomprehensibility.
*a. 5 to 15   c. 10 to 20
b. 10   d. 5 to 10

17. In grouped frequency distributions, we typically use interval sizes of _____.
a. 2 or 3   *c. 2, 3, or multiples of 5
b. 5 or 10   d. none of the above

18. In a grouped frequency distribution, the conventional starting point for the lowest interval is the closest number evenly divisible by the interval size that is equal to or less than the _____:
a. highest score   c. interval size
*b. lowest score   d. real limits of the score

Questions 19-20 refer to the following frequency distribution:

X	f
10	2
9	3
8	3
7	5
6	2
5	3
4	0
3	2

19. What is the relative frequency associated with a score of 9?
*a. .15   b. .30   c. .45   d. 3

20. What is the cumulative frequency associated with a score of 6?
a. 2   b. 5   *c. 7   d. 13

21. A frequency distribution for qualitative variables would include all but which of the following?
a. frequencies
*b. cumulative frequency
c. relative frequency
d. percentages

22. Cumulative relative frequencies are not appropriate for ____ variables.
a. quantitative
*b. qualitative
c. discrete

23. In frequency distributions for qualitative variables, the concepts of cumulative frequencies, cumulative relative frequencies, and cumulative percentages:
a. are still applicable
b. are mathematically different
c. are functionally equivalent
*d. are not applicable

24. A(n) ____ is a case or a set of cases that shows a very extreme score relative to the majority of cases in the data set.
*a. outlier
b. anomaly
c. residual
d. deviant case

25. In a frequency histogram, the horizontal dimension is called the ____, and the vertical dimension is called the ____.
a. X axis; Y axis
b. abscissa; ordinate
c. ordinate; abscissa
*d. a and b

26. In a stem and leaf plot of IQ scores, the digits representing the number of "hundreds" and "tens" are the ____.
a. leaf
b. base
c. stem
*d. b and c

27. The major difference between a frequency histogram and a bar graph is that, in a bar graph, the bars are drawn such that they:
a. represent quantitative variables
b. represent continuous variables
*c. do not touch one another
d. do touch one another

28. Because frequency graphs can be misleading depending on how the abscissa and ordinate are formatted, behavioral scientists have adopted a _____.
*a. "two-thirds high" rule
b. "ordinate only" rule
c. "formatted ordinate" rule
d. "one-third high" rule

29. In a cumulative frequency graph, the cumulative frequency curve will always _____ or _____ as it moves from left to right.
a. be variable; decrease
*b. remain level; increase
c. increase; decrease
d. remain level; decrease

30. The horizontal dimension of a frequency histogram is called a(n) _____.
*a. abscissa
b. Y axis
c. ordinate
d. frequency line

31. The vertical dimension of a frequency histogram is called _____.
*a. an ordinate
b. an X axis
c. an abscissa
d. none of the above

32. Frequency graphs typically plot the frequency of a score along the _____.
a. abscissa
*b. ordinate
c. X axis
d. all of the above

33. A frequency polygon is typically used when the variable of interest is _____.
a. discrete
b. nominal
c. qualitative
*d. continuous

34. If you want to graph a variable that is qualitative in nature, then you should use _____.
*a. a bar graph
b. a histogram
c. a frequency polygon
d. it doesn't matter

35. Quantitative variables can be graphed using _____.
a. frequency polygons
b. bar graphs
c. frequency histograms
*d. both a and c

36. A major difference between bar graphs and histograms is that _____.
a. bar graphs exhibit only discrete data
b. histograms use qualitative data
*c. bar graphs separate the bars
d. histograms separate the bars

37. In frequency histograms, the frequencies associated with score values are labeled along the _____, and the score values are labeled along the _____.
a. abscissa; ordinate
b. bottom; side
*c. ordinate; abscissa
d. horizontal axis; vertical axis

38. In a frequency polygon, the vertical bar denotes the _____, and the horizontal bar denotes the _____.
*a. frequencies; variable values
b. variable values; frequencies
c. abscissa; ordinate
d. frequencies; ordinate

39. In a histogram, the horizontal bar denotes the _____, and the vertical bar denotes the _____.
a. frequencies; ordinate
c. abscissa; variable values
*b. variable values; frequencies
d. frequencies; variable values

40. To produce a probability distribution of some variable, that variable must have the properties of being _____ and _____.
a. continuous; inclusive
b. mutually inclusive; discrete
c. exhaustive; inclusive
*d. mutually exclusive; exhaustive

41. Probability distributions for continuous variables are conceptualized in terms of _____.
a. exact probability calculations
b. precise calculations
c. mutually exclusive scores
*d. probability density functions

42. A probability density function _____.
a. can be graphically represented as a bar graph
b. can be used only to represent variables that are measured on a ratio curve
*c. is a smooth curve including all possible values of a continuous variable
d. is always bell-shaped

43. Which of the following types of variables cannot be specified by listing possible values of the variable with corresponding probabilities?
a. qualitative
b. discrete
*c. continuous
d. all of the above

44. Given a distribution of scores, the probability of randomly selecting a given score from that distribution equals the _____ of that score.
a. cumulative frequency
b. cumulative relative frequency
c. frequency
*d. relative frequency

45. When the potential values for a qualitative or discrete variable are _____ and _____, then the probabilities associated with the individual score values will represent a probability distribution with respect to that variable.
*a. mutually exclusive; exhaustive
b. mutually exclusive; nonexhaustive
c. nominal; cumulative
d. normally distributed; exhaustive

46. Statisticians conceptualize a probability distribution of a _____ in terms of a probability density function.
a. qualitative variable
b. discrete variable
c. density slope
*d. continuous variable

47. The total area under the _____ represents _____.
a. density area; 1.0
b. density curve; 10.0
*c. density curve; 1.0
d. density area; 100%

48. _____ are derived by making assumptions and representing those assumptions mathematically.
a. Empirical distributions
*b. Theoretical distributions
c. Assumptive distributions
d. Realistic distributions

49. All distributions in the family of _____ distributions are symmetrical and characterized by a "bell shape."
a. empirical
b. theoretical
c. actual
*d. normal

50. Which is not true of a normal distribution?
a. It is bell-shaped.
b. It is theoretical in nature.
c. It is symmetrical.
*d. It is empirically derived.

Chapter 3: Measures of Central Tendency and Variability

Comments to Instructors

This chapter introduces a number of symbols ($\overline{X}$, Mdn, IQR, SS, s^2, s) and I forewarn my students that it is crucial to become fluent in the use of them. This is true in this chapter as well as later chapters. As before, I find the material in this chapter is easy to teach and that students usually don't encounter problems mastering it.

Examples for Class

To illustrate the calculation of a mean, median, and mode, I use two small data sets of 12 criminals who have been convicted of rape. I report the number of years that they have been sentenced to serve in prison:

$$2, 3, 4, 5, 5, 7, 8, 9, 9, 10, 11, 11$$

and the number of years that they actually serve:

$$1, 2, 2, 3, 3, 3, 3, 3, 4, 6, 6, 6$$

You can position these data for students in the context of a criminologist studying prison life. The mode for the first distribution is 5, 9, and 11 (there are three modes) and the mode for the second distribution is 3. This allows me to illustrate the notion of multi-modes. The median for the first set of scores is 7.5. This value maps roughly onto national estimates of sentence length made by the FBI (for the year, 1992). To illustrate the median for an odd number of cases, I simply drop a score of 11 and re-compute it. To illustrate the median when there are ties in the middle, I use the second set of data. It equals 3.10. Again, the median value roughly maps onto national estimates of actual time served.

I use the above two data sets to illustrate the calculation of the mean, the IQR, the sum of squares, variance, and standard deviation. Note that there is less variability in the scores for time served versus time sentenced and I show how this is reflected in the measures of variability when I present the data to the class. I chose the scores of the second set so that the mean would equal 3.5. This permits me to illustrate the use of fractions in the calculation of squared deviation scores. For the two sets of data, here are the values of the core statistics

	Time Sentenced	Time Served
Mode	5	3
Median	7.50	3.10
$\overline{X}$	7.00	3.50
Range	9	5
IQR	4	1
SS	108	31
s^2	9.00	2.58
s	3.00	1.61

The above data can also be used to illustrate the graphing techniques discussed in the chapter.

Answers to Selected Exercises

4. 5

5. $\overline{X} = 21.048$ Mode = 20   Median = 21

19. 49

22. $\Sigma X^2 = 465$ $(\Sigma X)^2 = 3249$

25.   Set I
   Range = 290
   SS = 69256
   Variance = 8657
   Standard Deviation = 93.04

   Set II
   Range = 2
   SS = 4
   Variance = .50
   Standard Deviation = .71

32. Company A   Company B

     $\overline{X} = 4.0$ $\overline{X} = 4.0$
     $s = 1.291$ $s = 0$

47. b

Test Questions

1. The term "central tendency" refers to _____.
a. an average
b. a score around which other scores tend to cluster
*c. both a and b
d. neither a nor b

2. _____ refers to the "average" score in a set of scores.
*a. central tendency   c. average deviation
b. variability   d. none of the above

3. Measures of _____ indicate the extent to which scores within a set differ from one another.
a. central tendency   c. differential tendency
*b. variability   d. none of the above

4. The mode of a distribution of scores:
a. is the most easily computed index of central tendency
b. is simply the score that occurs most frequently
c. has the highest "peak" in a graph of a distribution of scores
*d. all of the above

5. The major problem with the mode as a measure of central tendency is that:
a. there can be only one modal score
*b. there can be more than one modal score
c. the mode is insensitive to variability
d. the mode is insensitive to kurtosis

6. Which of the following statements is true of the mode of any set of scores?
*a. It is the score which occurs most frequently.
b. It is always less than the mean.
c. Both a and b.
d. Neither a nor b.

7. Consider the following scores achieved by subjects taking a standard IQ test: 68, 83, 93, 100, 101, 103, 106, 120. The mode is _____.
a. 93
b. 101
c. 97.88
*d. none of the above

8. If you were to randomly select one score from a set of scores, the score most likely to be selected _____.
a. would be equal to the medium of the set of scores
*b. would be equal to the mode of the set of scores
c. would be equal to the mean of the set of scores
d. can vary with the numerical values of the individual scores

9. Compute the median of the following set of scores: 106, 106, 109, 110, 113, 121, 121.
a. 109.5
*b. 110
c. 106 and 121
d. cannot be determined from information given

10. Eight psychology students took a well-known I.Q. test and achieved the following scores: 96, 98, 108, 110, 115, 120, 121, 142. The median score for these students is _____.
a. 96
*b. 112.5
c. 113.5
d. 115

11. Which of the following statements is true of a median score?
a. It divides a distribution in half.
b. It may not have been a score actually achieved.
*c. Both a and b.
d. Neither a nor b.

12. Suppose a researcher was interested in determining the effect of an experimental drug on the lifespan of laboratory rats. Shown below is a summary of the lifespans, in months, for laboratory animals administered the drug. Compute the median number of months the animals survived.

Number of months	Number of animals surviving
6	10
5	10
4	15
3	25
2	25
1	5
0	10

a. 3.1 b. 25 c. 3.0 *d. 2.9

13. The _____ is the point in the distribution of scores that divides the distribution into two equal parts.
a. mean
b. mode
*c. median
d. standard deviation

14. When there is an even number of scores, the median is the _____.
a. most frequently occurring score
b. arithmetic average of the scores
*c. arithmetic average of the two middle scores
d. arithmetic average of the two most extreme scores

15. As a measure of central tendency, the median _____ the absolute difference between it and the scores in the distribution.
*a. minimizes
b. maximizes
c. summarizes
d. none of the above

16. The _____ is simply the arithmetic average of a set of scores.
a. median
*b. mean
c. mode
d. standard deviation

17. The mean is computed by summing all of the scores and then dividing the sum by the:
a. standard deviation
b. mean divisor
*c. total number of scores
d. average number of scores

18. The sum of signed deviations about the mean will always equal _____.
a. 10
b. -10
c. the sum of squares
*d. 0

19. Most of the inferential statistics used by behavioral scientists make use of the ___ as a measure of central tendency.
*a. mean
b. median
c. mode
d. all are used with equal frequency

20. The mean, median, and mode are applicable to:
a. continuous variables only
b. discrete variables only
*c. continuous and discrete variables
d. interval and ratio level variables only

21. The mean of a set of scores is best described as _____.
*a. a simple arithmetic average
b. an arithmetic average weighted by the number of subjects
c. usually equal to the mode
d. relatively free of the effects of extreme values

22. A teacher wants to determine the mean score of students taking a newly developed test. Her students scored as follows: 40, 45, 60, 65, 70, 70, 70, 80, 90, 100. Compute the mean for the class.
*a. 69
b. 70
c. 69.5
d. none of the above

23. If a researcher were to subtract the mean of a distribution from each score in that distribution and add the differences, the resulting value would _____.
a. be equal to the median
*b. always be zero
c. be greater than the mode
d. depend upon the scores that make up the distribution

24. If you subtract the mean from each score in a distribution, you would obtain a set of _____.
*a. signed deviation scores
b. standard individual deviation scores
c. absolute deviation scores
d. signed discrepancy scores

25. The median _____ the sum of the _____ deviations.
a. minimizes; signed
*b. minimizes; unsigned
c. maximizes; signed
d. maximizes; unsigned

26. After giving a test to all members of his college class, a professor found that the scores totaled 1500 and the mean was 75. How many students took the test?
a. 25
*b. 20
c. 22
d. cannot be determined without additional information

27. In a normal distribution, the _____.
a. mean is usually higher than the mode
b. median is usually lower than the mean
c. mean, median, and mode might be equal
*d. mean, median, and mode are always equal

28. The _____ is the measure of central tendency that is most sensitive to extreme values in a distribution.
a. mode
b. standard deviation
c. median
*d. mean

29. The extent to which scores in a distribution differ is indicated by _____.
a. measures of central tendency
*b. measures of variability
c. the result of subtracting each score from the median
d. the average of the mean and the standard deviation

30. Given the data set 8, 8, 8, 7, 5, 6, 2, 2, what is the range?
a. 8
b. 2
c. 5.75
*d. 6

31. The _____ is the highest score minus the lowest score.
a. variance
b. standard deviation
c. interquartile range
*d. range

32. The _____ is the difference between the highest and lowest scores after the top 25% of the scores and the bottom 25% of the scores have been eliminated from the data.
a. range
*b. interquartile range
c. intermediate range
d. intertertial range

33. The interquartile range has been criticized because it does not take into account:
a. the sum of squares
*b. all of the scores in the distribution
c. none of the above

34. Compute the sum of squares for the following data set: 2, 2, 3, 6, 9, 13, 14.
*a. 156
c. 7
b. 22.28
d. none of the above

35. SS is the _____.
a. sum of standard scores
*b. sum of squared deviations from the mean
c. sum of standard deviations from the mean
d. sum of standard deviations from the median

36. If SS for 30 students is 900, what is the variance?
a. 5.47
b. more than 30
c. less than 30
*d. exactly 30

37. The positive square root of the variance is the _____.
a. root square mean
*b. standard deviation
c. variance square root
d. absolute squared deviation

38. Considering the distribution -2, -4, -6, -8, -10, the SS is _____.
*a. 40
b. 8
c. -40
d. -8

39. Using the data set for question 34, compute the standard deviation.
a. 20
b. 40
c. -6.32
*d. 2.83

40. Distributions of scores can have _____.
a. identical standard deviations with different means
b. identical means with different standard deviations
*c. either a or b
d. neither a nor b

41. The sum of squared deviations from the _____ will always be _____ the sum of squared deviations around any other value.
a. median; less than
b. mode; equal to
c. mean; greater than
*d. mean; less than

42. One problem with the sum of squares as an index of variability is that its size depends not only on the amount of _____ among the scores, but also on the _____ of scores.
*a. variability; number
b. skewness; kurtosis
c. error; number
d. none of the above

43. The variance is the:
*a. sum of squares divided by N
b. the average squared deviation from the mean
c. a and b
d. neither a nor b

44. The standard deviation is the:
a. square root of the sum of squares
*b. positive square root of the variance
c. negative square root of the variance
d. sum of squares divided by N

45. The best answer to the question, "What value indicates a large standard deviation?" is:
a. any value greater than 10.00
b. any value greater than 100.00
c. it depends on the variability
*d. it depends on what is being measured

46. Distributions of scores can have:
a. identical variabilities but very different central tendencies
b. identical central tendencies but very different variabilities
*c. a and b
d. neither a nor b

47. In positively skewed distributions, most scores occur _____ the mean and only a relatively few extreme scores occur _____ it.
*a. below; above
b. at; above
c. below; above
d. at; below

48. The mean of a _____ skewed distribution will always be _____ than the median.
a. positively; less
*b. negatively; less
c. negatively; greater
d. normal; less

49. If a distribution is less peaked than another, it is said to be more _____; if it is more peaked than another, it is said to be more _____.
a. skewed; variable
b. leptokurtic; variable
*c. platykurtic; leptokurtic
d. leptokurtic; platykurtic

50. _____ refer(s) to the tendency for scores to cluster on one side of the mean in some distributions.
a. Unbalancing
*b. Skewness
c. Both a and b
d. Neither a nor b

51. Use of Greek notation implies that the parameters describe _____ characteristics.
a. sample
b. normally distributed
c. random
*d. population

52. When presenting measures of central tendency and variability, most researchers report _____ and _____, which are the most _____ descriptive statistics.
*a. means; standard deviations; frequently used
b. means; standard deviations; precisely defined
c. means; standard deviations; generally accurate
d. none of the above

Chapter 4: Percentiles, Percentile Ranks, Standard Scores, and the Normal Distribution

Comments to Instructors

Chapters 2 and 3 focus on statistical indices for describing an entire set of scores. By contrast, this chapter focuses on how to interpret a *single* score within a distribution of scores. Some students miss this change in focus and I find it helpful to emphasize the change.

Examples for Class

To illustrate percentiles and percentile ranks, I use an example on body image. For a sample of 300 college students, I calculated a difference score in which a woman's self report of her ideal weight is subtracted from a measure of the woman's actual weight. Thus, larger scores indicate that the women is heavier than what she perceives as her ideal weight. Here is a table that can be used to calculate different percentiles and percentile ranks:

Value	f	rf	cf	crf
15.00	14	.047	300	1.000
14.00	14	.047	286	.953
13.00	24	.080	272	.907
12.00	30	.100	248	.827
11.00	37	.123	218	.727
10.00	40	.133	181	.603
9.00	48	.160	141	.470
8.00	26	.087	93	.310
7.00	26	.087	67	.223
6.00	18	.060	41	.136
5.00	10	.033	23	.076
4.00	6	.020	13	.043
3.00	2	.007	7	.023
2.00	1	.003	5	.016
1.00	3	.010	4	.013
.00	1	.003	1	.003

The mean of the above data is 9.67 and the standard deviation is 2.92. I use this information to illustrate examples with standard scores.

To illustrate the use of standard scores in conjunction with a normal distribution, I use an example with a test designed to measure procrastination tendencies. I explain that the test contains 20 statements and that individuals can respond to each statement on a five point agree-disagree scale. Each item is scored from 1 to 5, with higher scores indicating a response that indicates higher levels of a tendency to procrastinate. The items scores are summed, yielding a test that ranges from 5 to 100. I explain that the scores are approximately normally distributed with a mean of 50 and a standard deviation of 5. I state that an individual has a score of 57 and then use the above information to gain perspectives on where this score falls within the distribution (e.g., I calculate the proportion of scores that are less than 57). Many other examples can be developed from this. The example can also be used to illustrate T scores.

Answers to Selected Exercises

3. IQR = 3.24 - 4.625 = 1.385

5. 98.0

6. 2.0

10. a. -1.132   d. -1.00
    b. 1.60   e. 2.00
    c. 2.736   f. 1.948

12. -1.802

21. a. -1.848   d. -2.00
    b. .758   e. 2.172
    c. .323   f. 1.413

24. a. .50   d. .6179
    b. .50   e. .6915
    c. .1934 f. .3085

32. c

42. a

43. d

Test Questions

1. The percentage of scores in a distribution that occur at or below a given value is the ____ of that value.
   a. relative percentage
   *c. percentile rank
   b. standard deviation
   d. relative distribution

2. A survey finds that 50% of college students spend 10 hours or less on homework weekly. The percentile rank of ____ is ____.
   a. 50; 10
   c. 50; 50
   *b. 10; 50
   d. cannot be determined

3. The score value corresponding to a given percentile rank is referred to as a(n) ____.
   a. optimal value
   c. standard score
   b. median value
   *d. percentile

4. A survey finds that 80% of high school students scored at least 75 on a given intelligence test. The 80th ____ is ____.
   *a. percentile; 75
   c. score; 75%
   b. value; 75
   d. percentile; 25

5. In a frequency distribution, the term designating the score corresponding to the 50th percentile is known as the ____.
   a. mean
   c. mode
   *b. median
   d. standard deviation

6. The percentage of scores in the distribution that occur at or below a given value, X, is the _____ of that value.
a. standard score
*b. percentile rank
c. percentile
d. rank

7. The score value corresponding to a given percentile rank is referred to as a _____.
a. z-score
b. percentage
*c. percentile
d. none of the above

8. The median corresponds to the _____ percentile.
*a. 50th
b. 75th
c. average
d. standard

9. A percentile rank reflects a(n) _____ measure of relative standing.
a. nominal
*b. ordinal
c. interval
d. ratio

10. The number of standard deviation units that a score falls above or below the mean is represented by the _____.
a. median frequency
b. percentile rank
c. relative frequency
*d. standard score

11. A standard score converts a score from its original, or raw form to a form that takes into consideration its standing relative to the _____ and _____ of the entire distribution of scores.
a. percentile; percentile rank
b. percentile; standard deviation
c. mean; percentile rank
*d. mean; standard deviation

12. A standard score represents the number of _____ that a score falls above or below the mean.
a. units
b. percentile units
*c. standard deviation units
d. standard score units

13. A _____ standard score indicates that the original score is _____ than the mean.
a. positive; greater
b. negative; less
*c. a and b
d. neither a nor b

14. A standard score of _____ indicates that the original score is equal to the mean.
*a. 0
b. +1.00
c. -1.00
d. 1.96

15. The _____ of a set of standard scores is always equal to 0.
a. standard deviation
b. mean
c. sum
*d. b and c

16. The _____ and the _____ of a set of standard scores is always equal to 1.00.
a. mean; variance
*b. standard deviation; variance
c. variance; range
d. mean; standard deviation

17. One important use of standard scores is to compare scores on distributions that have different _____ and _____.
a. medians and IQRs
b. standard deviations and variances
*c. means and standard deviations
d. none of the above

18. All normal distributions are:
a. asymmetrical about the mean
*b. characterized by a "bell shape"
c. positively skewed
d. a and b

19. In all normal distributions, the mean, the median, and the mode are all:
a. unequal to each other
b. standardized to 1.00
c. evenly distributed
*d. equal to each other

20. All normal distributions are _____ in nature.
a. asymmetrical
*b. theoretical
c. leptokurtic
d. all of the above

21. One property of normal distributions is that the proportion of scores that occur _____ is the same in all such distributions.
a. above or below a given standard score
b. between two specified standard scores
*c. a and b
d. a only

22. It is always the case that _____ of the scores in a normal distribution occur above the mean and _____ of the scores in a normal distribution occur below the mean.
*a. .50; .50
b. .75; .25
c. all; none
d. .25; .75

23. In a normal distribution, approximately _____ of all scores fall between standard scores of -1 and +1.
a. 50%
*b. 68%
c. 95%
d. 99%

24. In a normal distribution, approximately 95% of all scores fall between standard scores of _____.
a. -1 and +1
b. 0 and +2
*c. -2 and +2
d. -3 and +3

25. In a normal distribution, approximately _____ of all scores fall between standard scores of -3 and +3.
a. 50%
b. 68%
c. 95%
*d. 99%

26. The proportion of scores occurring between standard scores of 0 and -1 is _____ the proportion of scores occurring between standard scores of 0 and +1.
*a. equal to
b. less than
c. greater than
d. less than or equal to

27. A _____ score in a _____ distribution is referred to as a z score.
a. raw; normal
*b. standard; normal
c. raw; binomial
d. standard; binomial

28. The process of standardizing scores _____ the basic shape of the distribution.
a. normalizes
b. changes
*c. does not change
d. reveals

29. A set of scores that is positively skewed will _____ after they have been converted to standard scores.
a. be normalized
b. become negatively skewed
*c. remain positively skewed
d. become platykurtic

37

30. Standardization _____ the central tendency and variability of the scores.
*a. affects
b. does not affect
c. minimizes
d. maximizes

31. Standardization _____ the skewness and kurtosis of the scores.
a. affects
*b. does not affect
c. minimizes
d. maximizes

32. John scores an 85 on his psychology exam. The other relevant characteristics of the distribution are as follows: $\overline{X} = 75$, $s^2 = 4$. What is John's standard score?
*a. 2.5   b. -2.5   c. .625   d. -.625

33. When a standard score is 0, the original (raw) score is equal to the _____ of the distribution.
a. mode
b. median
*c. mean
d. standard deviation

34. The sum of a set of standard scores for a distribution will _____ equal 0.
*a. always
b. never
c. sometimes
d. cannot be determined

35. The mean of a set of standard scores for a given distribution is _____.
a. 100   b. 50   c. 1   *d. 0

36. The standard deviation of a set of standard scores in a distribution is _____.
a. 100   b. 50   *c. 1   d. 0

37. In a normal distribution, approximately _____ of all scores fall between the standard scores of -1 and +1.
a. 50%   *b. 68%   c. 33%   d. 25%

38. In a normal distribution, approximately _____ of all scores fall between the standard scores of -1.96 and +196.
* a. 95%   b. 75%   c. 66%   d. 50%

39. Another name for a standard score in a normal distribution is _____
*a. z score
b. percentile rank
c. z score in any distribution
d. cumulative relative frequency

40. Given an approximately normal distribution of test scores with $\mu = 75$, $\sigma = 25$, what test (raw) score would correspond to a z score of 1.5?
*a. 77.5
b. 87.5
c. 76.5
d. cannot be determined

41. Given a normal distribution, what z score would correspond to the 95th percentile?
a. 1.96   b. 1   c. 2   *d. 1.645

42. Given a normal distribution, what z score would correspond to the 50th percentile?
a. +1   b. -1   c. 0   *d. +.5

43. For a T score with a mean of 50 and a standard deviation of 10, the T score equivalent to a standard score of 2.5 is ___.
a. 2.5   b. 52.5   c. 3.5   *d. 75

Given a normal distribution of test scores with $\overline{X} = 80$, $s^2 = 49$, use this information to answer Questions 44-46.

44. What is the z score corresponding to a test score of 70?
*a. -1.43   b. 1.43   c. -2.1   d. 22

45. What is the z score corresponding to a test score of 95?
a. .31   b. -.31   *c. 2.14   d. -2.14

46. What percentage of scores fall between the test scores of 70 and 95?
a. 25%   b. 64%   c. 97%   *d. 91%

47. Suppose an approximately normal distribution of doctors' salaries finds μ = $150,000 and σ = $25,000. What salary level would define the 77th percentile?
a. $180,000
c. $175,000
*b. $168,000
d. $158,250

48. The ____ of the standard score formula represents the number of units the score is above or below the mean.
*a. numerator
c. obtained value
b. denominator
d. none of the above

49. A negative standard score indicates that the ____ was below the mean of the distribution.
*a. raw score
c. standard deviation
b. sum of squares
d. none of the above

50. Percentile rank reflects a(n) ____ measure of relative standing.
a. nominal
c. ratio
b. interval
*d. ordinal

51. Approximately what proportion of a normal distribution lies between the z scores of +.66 and +1.55?
a. 57%   b. 63%   *c. 68%   d. 32%

52. John scored an 85 on his most recent psychology exam. Which of the following distributions would John least prefer (assuming he wishes to perform as well as possible, and higher test scores are more favorable)?
*a. $\overline{X}$ = 80, s = 104
c. $\overline{X}$ = 70, s = 15
b. $\overline{X}$ = 80, s = 5
d. $\overline{X}$ = 70, s = 10

Use the following information to answer Questions 31-37.

An instructor has given his final exam, and scores are approximately normally distributed. Nancy scores a 90 and Ronald scores a 75. The characteristics of the distribution are as follows: $\overline{X}$ = 85, s^2 = 36.

53. What is Nancy's z score?
a. .14   b. -.14   *c. .83   d. -.83

40

54. What is Ronald's z score?
a. 1.67   *b. -1.67   c. .28   d. -.28

55. What is Nancy's T score (for a mean of 50 and a standard deviation of 10)?
a. 51.4   b. 5.14   c. 5.83   *d. 58.3

56. What is Ronald's T score (for a mean of 50 and a standard deviation of 10)?
*a. 33.3   b. 63.7   c. 52.8   d. 47.2

57. What is Nancy's approximate percentile rank?
a. 59   b. 30   c. 41   *d. 80

58. What is Ronald's approximate percentile rank?
a. .91   c. 45
*b. 5   d. none of the above

59. Approximately what percentage of scores falls at or between Nancy's and Ronald's scores?
*a. 75%   b. 35%   c. 11%   d. 50%

60. A z score converts the raw score to a form that takes into consideration its standing relative to the ___ and ___ of the entire distribution of scores.
a. median; standard deviation
*b. mean; standard deviation
c. mean; variance
d. median; interquartile range

61. A raw score of 96 on two separate examinations may have different ___ depending on the mean and standard deviations of each examination.
a. percentile ranks   c. percentiles
b. standard scores   *d. all of the above

62. Gary is told that his percentile rank on the law school admissions exam is 87. This indicates that 87% of students taking this exam scored ____ Gary.
a. higher than
b. higher than or equal to
c. lower than
*d. lower than or equal to

63. Approximately what raw score in a normal distribution would correspond to a z score of 1.56 with $\overline{X} = 75$ and $s^2 = 4$?
*a. 78   b. 81   c. 72   d. 69

64. Percentile ranks must always be interpreted relative to the ____ upon which the scores are based.
*a. group
b. scale
c. percentiles
d. all of the above

Chapter 5: Pearson Correlation and Regression: Descriptive Aspects

Comments to Instructors

This chapter again shifts the focus from descriptive indices of data on a single variable (Chapters 2 and 3) and interpretation of a score within a distribution (Chapter 4) to the analysis of the relationship between two variables. This shift in focus is important to emphasize to students, otherwise they may become confused.

A common error that students make in this chapter is to think that a negative correlation coefficient implies a weaker linear relationship than a positive correlation coefficient (e.g., -.75 is weaker than .75). Another concept that students tend to have a difficult time with is the interpretation of the standard error of estimate. What is a large value and what is a small value? I make sure to provide them with many examples on this.

At this point, the word "standard" appears in several of the terms we have used: standard deviation, standard score, standard normal distribution, and standard error of estimate. Each of these terms refers to something different, but students start to confuse them (and it only gets worse in later chapters!). I find it useful to point this out to students.

Examples for Class

In order to review the linear model, I find that the example from the main textbook using the amount of money paid as a function of the number of hours worked is quite effective. I use this in class, even though it is repetitious with the textbook.

To illustrate the calculation of the correlation coefficient and the calculation of a least squares regression equation, I use an example from developmental psychology focusing on child self reports of anxiety (i.e., in general, how anxious the child is) and mother reports of how anxious her child is. The literature suggests that there is only a moderate correlation between these alternative measures, and it is interesting to students to engage in a discussion as to why this may be the case, after the example has been developed and the statistics presented. Reasons include low reliability of the child measure, the fact that parents don't always understand the world of their child, the fact that parents don't see all of the experiences that a child has (e.g., in school and in other settings away from the home), and so on. I use an example with only 11 cases, so that the in-class computations are manageable. I frame the regression analysis in terms of trying to predict the child's report of anxiety from the mother report. I describe the child measure as consisting of 10 items, to which the child answers true or false (e.g., I get scared easily; I worry alot; I get nervous in school). Each item is scored 0 or 1, with a 1 indicating an "anxious" response. The item scores are summed to yield a score from 0 to 10, with higher scores indicating greater anxiety. The mother completes a comparable 10 item measure, but rephrased for the focus on the child (e.g., my child gets scared easily; my child worries alot; my child gets nervous in school). Scoring is the same as the child measure. Here are the data (where CR is the child report and MR is the mother report):

CR	MR	$\hat{Y}$	$Y-\hat{Y}$
3.00	1.00	4.33333	-1.33333
4.00	2.00	5.16667	-1.16667
5.00	3.00	6.00000	-1.00000
5.00	3.00	6.00000	-1.00000
6.00	5.00	7.66667	-1.66667
6.00	4.00	6.83333	-.83333
6.00	3.00	6.00000	.00000
7.00	2.00	5.16667	1.83333
7.00	3.00	6.00000	1.00000
8.00	3.00	6.00000	2.00000
9.00	4.00	6.83333	2.16667

The mean for CR is 6.00 and the mean for MR is 3.00. The sum of squares and standard deviation for CR is 30 and 1.65 and the corresponding values for MR are 12 and 1.04. The SCP is 10. The correlation between CR and MR is .527. The regression equation is

CR = 3.50 + .833 MR. The standard error of estimate is 1.40. The data can also be used to show a scatterplot.

Answers to Selected Exercises

13. $r = .18$

14. $r = -.62$

20. $\hat{Y} = 5.00 + .20X$

22. $\hat{Y} = 12.57 + (-.62)X$

23. a. 8.23
    b. 8.23
    c. 7.61

26. 0.86

39. b

41. c

Test Questions

1. The Pearson correlation technique may be used to measure _____ relationships when both variables are _____ in nature.
   a. curvilinear; qualitative   *c. linear; quantitative
   b. linear; qualitative   d. curvilinear; quantitative

2. The Pearson correlation may be used to determine the _____.
   *a. relationship between two variables
   b. variability between x and y scores
   c. curvilinear relationship between x and y
   d. predictive error between two scores

3. Research in the behavioral sciences is often concerned with _____ relationships.
a. qualified
b. unsystematic
*c. linear
d. all of the above

4. The _____ of a line indicates the number of units variable Y changes as variable X changes by 1 unit.
*a. slope
b. intercept
c. scatterplot
d. residual

5. A slope of _____ would be represented by a _____ line.
a. 1.0; nonlinear
*b. 0; horizontal
c. -1.0; horizontal
d. 1.0; horizontal

6. In the case of a _____ relationship, as scores on X increase, scores on Y also increase.
a. curvilinear
*b. positive
c. negative
d. constant

7. In the case of a negative relationship, as scores on X _____, scores on Y _____.
a. increase; stay the same
b. decrease; stay the same
c. decrease; decrease
*d. increase; decrease

8. The point at which a line intersects the Y axis when X = 0 is called the _____.
*a. intercept
b. slope
c. abscissa
d. a and c

9. The general form of the linear model is _____.
a. Y = bX + aX
*b. Y = a + bX
c. Y = b + a + X
d. Y = a + bX^2

10. If the value of variables X and Y are inversely related, then as a score on X _____ the value of a score on Y _____.
a. decreases; decreases
*c. increases; decreases
b. increases; increases
d. none of the above

11. If the values of the variables X and Y are directly related, then as a score in X _____ the value of a score in Y _____.
*a. increase; increases
b. increases; decreases
c. decreases; increases
d. none of the above

12. If grade point average (GPA) and number of hours partying were related according to the following linear model: GPA= 4.00 - .40 Hours, what GPA would you predict if you partied for 8 hours?
*a. .80
b. 2.20
c. 1.00
d. 3.60

13. The Pearson correlation coefficient can range from _____.
a. 0.0 to + 1.00
b. 1.00 to 100.00
*c. -1.00 to 1.00
d. 0.0 to ∞

14. The largest correlation coefficient that can be observed under any circumstance is _____.
a. 100%
*b. ±1.00
c. +1.00
d. unlimited

15. When there is no linear relationship, the z scores on X will _____.
*a. bear no relationship to the z scores on Y
b. vary in sign but not size with the z scores on Y
c. vary in size but not sign with the z scores on Y
d. none of the above

16. For a perfect negative linear relationship, the z scores for the Y and X variables will tend to have _____.
a. the same sign
b. all negative signs
*c. opposite signs
d. an inconsistent pairing of signs

17. For a perfect positive linear relationship, the z scores for the X and Y variables will tend to have _____.
a. opposite signs
b. all negative signs
c. only positive signs
*d. the same positive or negative signs

18. The sum of the cross products is a measure of _____.
*a. covariation between two sets of scores
b. variability between the X mean and the Y mean
c. sum of the squares for variable y multiplied by x values
d. the determination coefficient

19. Which of the following correlation values represents the strongest relationship?
a. .20   b. 60   *c. -.70   d. .09

20. Which of the following correlation scores represents the weakest relationship?
a. .40   b. .60   c. -.80   *d. .09

21. Which of the following linear relationships describes a situation in which the value of one variable increases as the value of the second variable decreases?
*a. -.35   b. .00   c. .75   d. 1.00

22. Which of the following linear relationships describes a situation in which the value of one variable decreases as the value of the second variable also decreases?
a. -.66   *b. .42   c. 1.10   d. -1.00

23. When a correlation is perfect and positive, which of the following holds true?
*a. r=1.00   c. r=-1.00
b. r=.00   d. both a and b

24. The sum of the cross-products indicates the extent to which two sets of scores _____.
a. vary from their mean
b. vary from the grand mean
*c. covary
d. depart from individual variation

25. In the study of traditionalism and ideal family size, a correlation of .66 was found indicating a _____.
*a. strong positive relationship
b. causal effect
c. weak positive relationship
d. strong causal effect

26. Correlational analysis frequently demonstrates how one variable _____.
a. causes the value of the other variable
b. is caused by the value of the other variable
c. is caused by a third variable
*d. may be related to another variable

27. The extent of _____ between two variables is indexed by a statistic known as the Pearson correlation coefficient.
*a. linear approximation   c. linear specification
b. nonlinear approximation   d. nonlinear specification

28. The magnitude of the correlation coefficient is indexed by its:
a. sign   *c. absolute value
b. slope   d. relative value

29. A correlation coefficient of _____ means the two variables form a perfect linear relationship.
a. +1.00   c. 0
b. -1.00   *d. a and b

30. In the case of a(n) _____ relationship, the standard scores on X and Y will have different signs but will be identical in size.
*a. perfect negative linear   c. imperfect negative nonlinear
b. prefect positive linear   d. imperfect negative linear

31. When two variables, X and Y, are correlated, it is possible that:
a. X causes Y
b. Y causes X
c. some other variable causes both X and Y
*d. all of the above

32. When some third variable is responsible for the correlation between X and Y, the correlation is said to be:
*a. spurious
b. false
c. nonlinear
d. moderate

33. Correlations for the types of variables studied any behavioral scientists will seldom exceed _____ and will often be considerably smaller.
a. -.80 or +.80
*b. -.40 or +.40
c. -.10 or +.10
d. -.05 or +.05

34. The technique which minimizes the squared vertical distances from the regression line to the data points is called the _____.
a. correlation line
*b. method of least squares
c. slope minimization technique
d. truncation of range technique

35. If two variables are perfectly correlated, then _____.
*a. all data points fall on the regression line
b. the average error in predicting scores is very large
c. the standard error of estimate is very large
d. an increase in x leads to no change in Y

36. The standard error of estimate is a useful index of _____.
*a. the (positive square root) average error across individuals
b. the slope
c. the rate of change of one variable compared to the other variable

37. If X helps to predict Y, then the standard deviation of Y _____.
*a. is larger than the standard error of estimate
b. is smaller than the standard error of estimate
c. will equal the standard error of estimate
d. will be independent of the standard error of estimate

Use the following data set and calculations to answer Questions 38-40.

Individual	X	Y
1	2	4
2	4	8
3	6	12
4	8	16
5	10	20

$SCP = 80$
$SS_Y = 160$
$SS_X = 40$

38. The correlation coefficient for the above is _____.
a. r=.75   b. r=-1.00   *c. 1.00   d. 0.00

39. The standard error of estimate is _____.
a. 1.00   c. insufficient data
*b. 0.00   d. 1%

40. The regression equation for the prediction of Y values is _____.
a. Y=X   c. Y=2X+2
b. Y=.5X   *d. Y=2X

41. In least squares analysis, the slope and intercept are defined so as to minimize the _____ that the data points, considered collectively, are from the regression line.
a. vertical distances   *c. squared vertical distances
b. horizontal distances   d. squared horizontal distances

42. The criterion for deriving the values of the slope and intercept in a linear regression problem is formally known as the:
a. maximum likelihood criterion   *c. least squares criterion
b. oblique squares criterion   d. sum of squares criterion

43. When scores on Y are predicted from scores on X using a regression equation, the amount of error for a given individual can be represented by the discrepancy between that person's:
*a. actual and predicted Y scores   c. a and b
b. actual and predicted X scores   d. neither a nor b

44. The _____ represents an average error across individuals in predicting scores on Y from the regression equation.
a. standard deviation   c. standard estimate of error
*b. standard error of estimate   d. standard error of discrepancy

45. If X helps to predict Y, then the _____ will be smaller than the _____.
a. standard deviation of Y; standard estimate of error
b. standard error of estimate; sum of squares for Y
c. standard estimate of error; standard deviation of X
*d. standard error of estimate; standard deviation of Y

46. If two variables are related in a fashion that is nonlinear, Pearson correlation:
a. will always be negative
b. will be sensitive to this
*c. will not be sensitive to this
d. will always be positive

47. The regression equation for predicting X from Y _____ as the regression equation for predicting Y from X.
*a. is not the same
b. is exactly the same
c. gives the same results
d. b and c

48. From a conceptual perspective, the tradition is to designate the independent variable as the _____ variable and the dependent variable as the _____ variable.
a. linear; nonlinear
b. Y; X
c. standardized; unstandardized
*d. X; Y

49. When standard scores are used to calculate the regression equation, the intercept will always equal _____ and the slope will always equal _____.
a. 1.0; the correlation coefficient
*b. 0; the correlation coefficient
c. 1.0; 0
d. 0; 1.0

50. Outliers are most likely to raise interpretational complexities when:
*a. sample sizes are small
b. sample sizes are large
c. correlation coefficients are small
d. correlation coefficients are large

Chapter 6: Probability

Comments to Instructors

The material in this chapter is straightforward, although students often have trouble with the different counting rules. It is good to go over these many times. I like to use examples for the counting rules that focus on designing studies and the number of different ways that stimulus combinations or permutations can be constructed (e.g., if you are giving four measures of personality traits and want to control for order of administration effects, how many different orders are there for the four tests).

One of the most common mistakes that students make in this chapter is to confuse the concepts of simple probability, joint probability and conditional probability.

Examples for Class

To illustrate the concepts of probability using a contingency table, I use an example with AIDS testing. I tell students that a health psychologist was interested in cultural differences in the willingness to be tested for the AIDS virus. A random sample of inner city women who were undergoing a pregnancy test were offered to be given a test for HIV infection. Here are the data:

	Agreed to take test	Refused to take test	Sum
African American	35	65	100
Hispanic	17	13	30
Caucasian	28	42	70
Sum	80	120	

These data can be used to calculate probabilities of simple events (e.g., the probability that a woman will agree to take an HIV test), conditional events (e.g., the probability that a woman will agree to take the HIV test given that she is African American), joint events (e.g., the probability that the women is an African American who agrees to take the HIV test), and so on.

For the binomial expression, you can use an example in which you are trying to measure how knowledgeable that pregnant women are about HIV transmission from mother to babies and the implications of having a baby who is HIV infected. The researcher gives a 10 item test, with each question having a true-false answer. If a person has no knowledge whatsoever and responds randomly to the items, then the probability of a correct answer on any given item is 0.50, as is the probability of an incorrect answer. I then use the binomial expression to calculate the probabilities that such an individual would get 0 correct, 1 correct, 2 correct, and so on. One can test the null hypothesis that a person has no knowledge and is responding randomly to illustrate the hypothesis testing framework developed in the textbook.

Answers to Selected Exercises

3. 175

11. p(favors legal abortion) = .55
    p(opposes legal abortion) = .45
    p(Democrat) = .40
    p(Republican) = .40
    p(Independent) = .20

12. p(favors legal abortion | Democrat) = .80
    p(Democrat | favors legal abortion) = .582

13. p(Democrat) = .40
    p(Democrat | opposes legal abortion) = .178

14. p(Republican, favors legal abortion) = .08
    p(Independent, opposes legal abortion) = .05

16. p(Republican or favors legal abortion) = .87
    p(Independent or opposes legal abortion) = .60

18. .12

19. .859

25. 120

27. a. 6   b. 4

29. 140608

35. $\mu = 124.8$
    $\sigma = 4.996$

39. c

41. a

43. b

45. b

Test Questions

1. According to the classical view of probability theory, the probability of event A equals ____.
a. the number of total observations/the number of events favoring A
*b. The number of events favoring A/the total number of possible observations
c. the number of events favoring A
d. 1 - the number of events favoring A/the total number of possible events

2. The outcome of a trial according to probability theory is a(n) ____.
a. conditional probability   *c. event
b. marginal frequency   d. joint probability

3. In probability theory, when two outcomes cannot occur simultaneously they are ____.
a. conditional probabilities
c. mutually exhaustive
*b. mutually exclusive
d. exhaustive

4. In the language of probability theory, the act of flipping a coin is called a(n) ____ and each unique outcome is called a(n) ____.
a. observation; trial
*b. trial; event
c. event; observation
d. none of the above.

5. The probability of an event, A, is formally defined as the number of observations favoring event A divided by the:
*a. total number of possible observations
b. total number of possible events
c. proportion of observations
d. proportion of events

6. In a population consisting of 60 males and 40 females, the probability of randomly selecting a male is:
a. 6%
*c. .60
b. .06
d. undefined

7. Each unique combination of variables in a contingency table is referred to as a:
a. marginal frequency
c. column
b. expected value
*d. cell

8. Two outcomes are said to be ____ if it is impossible for both outcomes to occur simultaneously for a given individual.
*a. mutually exclusive
b. mutually conditional
c. mutually distributed
d. mutually impossible

9. Given a set of outcomes that are mutually exclusive and exhaustive, the sum of the probabilities of the outcomes will always equal:
a. 100
b. .01
c. .10
*d. 1.0

Use the following data to answer Questions 10-16.

A researcher wanted to compare eye color distributions of babies born with a birth defect with babies who did not have the birth defect. 26 babies with the defect were matched on gender, race, and age with 52 babies without the defect. The frequency of different eye colors as a function of the presence or absence of the defects was as follows:

		Eye Color	
Group	Dark	Medium	Light
Defect	1	6	19
No Defect	15	13	24

10. The marginal frequencies for eye color are
a. 26 and 52
*b. 16, 19, 43
c. 78
*d. 156

11. The values entered within the table (that is, 1, 6, 19, 15, 13, 24) are called ____.
*a. cell frequencies
b. marginal frequencies
c. unit frequencies
d. cell probabilities

12. If a baby was randomly selected from those participating in the study, the likelihood of that baby having dark eyes is ____.
a. 1/16
b. 35/78
*c. 16/78
d. 1/26 + 15/52

57

13. If a baby were randomly selected from the study, what is the probability of that baby having light eyes?
a. .43   b. .19   c. .24   *d. .55

14. What is the probability that a baby has dark eyes given that the baby has the birth defect?
*a. .04   b. .06   c. .01   d. .61

15. A _____ probability indicates the likelihood that an event will occur given that some other event occurs.
a. joint
*b. conditional
c. simple
d. combination

16. The probability of the number of observations favoring both events A and B, divided by the total number of observations, is called a _____ probability.
a. conditional
b. binomial
*c. joint
d. simple

17. The probability of observing at least one of two events [for example, p(A or B)] is _____.
a. p(A,B) - p(A)
b. p(A,B) - p(B)
c. p(A)p(B)
*d. p(A) + p(B) - p(A,B)

18. If events A and B are independent, then _____.
*a. p(A|B) = p(A)
c. p(B|A) = p(A|B)
c. p(A) = (B)
d. none of the above

19. A _____ indicates the likelihood that an event will occur given that some other event occurs.
a. probability distribution
*b. conditional probability
c. marginal probability
d. mutually exclusive probability

20. The statement "Given that a person is satisfied with his job, what is the probability that he is satisfied with his marriage?" is an example of a(n):
a. hypothesis
*b. conditional probability
c. independent event
d. a and c

21. Even though two events are related (nonindependent), this does not necessarily mean that:
a. one is dependent on the other
*b. one causes the other
c. the joint probability is 0
d. a and c

22. The likelihood of observing each of two events is referred to as a:
a. hypothesis
b. binomial probability
c. conditional probability
*d. joint probability

23. The probability that an individual is satisfied with his marriage (event A) *and* satisfied with his job (event B) is an example of a _____.
*a. joint probability
b. conditional probability
c. marginal probability
d. mutually exclusive probability

24. In general notation, the probability of observing *at least one* of event A and event B is:
a. .50
b. $p(A \text{ or } B) = p(A) + p(B)$
c. $p(A \text{ or } B) = p(A) + p(B) + p(A, B)$
*d. $p(A \text{ or } B) = p(A) + p(B) - p(A, B)$

25. Let event *A* be "satisfied with one's marriage" and event *B* be "satisfied with one's job. The probability that someone is satisfied with *both* his marriage *and* his job is equal to:
a. p(A|B)
b. p(A,B)
c. p(B)p(A|B)
*d. b and c

26. Sampling without replacement causes the probability of randomly selecting additional cases from that population to____.
a. stay the same
b. increase
*c. decrease

27. The process of randomly selecting a case, taking some measurement of interest, and then returning the case to the population is called:
a. sampling without replacement
*b. sampling with replacement
c. sampling without error
d. sampling with error

28. In the case of sampling _____, the outcome of the first random selection in no way affects the outcome of the second random selection.
a. without replacement
*b. with replacement
c. with correction for continuity
d. without error

29. A(n) _____ of a set of objects or events is an *ordered* sequence.
a. enumeration
b. combination
*c. permutation
d. manipulation

30. A combination of a set of objects or events is a sequence in which the internal ordering of elements is:
a. systematic
b. predetermined
c. important
*d. irrelevant

31. A permutation of a set of objects or events ____.
*a. is an ordered sequence
b. is a sequence in which order doesn't matter
c. is a random selection of events
d. has fewer events than a combination

32. A counting rule that involves a set of objects of events in an ordered sequence is called a ____.
a. combination
b. conditional rule
c. binomial
*d. permutation

33. A set of objects that are arranged such that the internal order is irrelevant is called a ____.
*a. combination
b. binomial root
c. permutation
d. simple event

34. There are 6 students running for president at some college. The top 2 candidates are always declared winners and a run-off election is held to determine which of the two is the president. How many ways could 2 students be selected from among the first 6?
a. 30   b. 6!/2!   *c. 15   d. 6^3

35. In a horse race, people are allowed to bet on which horses will finish a race in positions 1, 2, or 3. If the field contained 7 horses, how many ways can 3 horses finish in the three positions?
a. 7!   *b. 210   c. 35   d. 3

36. Suppose you wanted a rat to learn a maze which included 3 choice points and each choice included 3 different directions. Assume only 1 choice can be correct at a time. What is the probability of a rat finding the goal without any errors?
a. 3!   b. 27   c. 1/9   *d. $.333^3$

37. In a binomial probability calculation, there are ____ possible outcomes.
a. many   b. N!   *c. two   d. N!/r!

38. Using the binomial expression to compute a probability requires ____.
*a. a sequence of n independent trials
b. more than 2 outcomes
c. that the probability of success = .5
d. that the probability of failure = 0

39. Suppose you are asked to toss 10 dimes and observe the number of heads. What is the likelihood of observing exactly 0 heads?
*a. .001   b. .50   c. 0   d. 1.0

40. A therapist claims that a particular technique has been successful in the treatment of eating disorders. You find out that only 7 out of 10 clients were actually helped. What is the probability of observing 7 successes if the probability of success = .5?
a. .7   b. .5   *c. .117   d. .77

41. If the probability of an experimental outcome that we observed was calculated to be less than .05 assuming the null hypothesis to be true, then we would ____.
a. accept the null hypothesis
*b. reject the null hypothesis
c. fail to reject the null hypothesis
d. change the alpha level

42. In factorial notation, the expression 6! equals:
a. 6 factorial
b. (6)(5)(4)(3)(2)(1) = 720
*c. a and b
d. neither a nor b

43. Assuming the null hypothesis is true, we can specify an ____ of an investigation.
*a. expected result
b. alternative result
c. improbable result
d. all of the above

44. If our observations are so discrepant from the expected result that the difference cannot be attributed to chance, we will _____ the null hypothesis.
a. accept
*b. reject
c. revise
d. restate

45. If the observed result of a study is similar enough to the outcome stated in the null hypothesis such that it can reasonably be attributed to chance, we will _____ the null hypothesis.
a. accept
b. reject
*c. fail to reject
d. revise

46. When the alpha level is .05, a result is defined as *non-chance* if the probability of obtaining that result, assuming the null hypothesis is true, is:
a. greater than .05
b. equal to .05
*c. less than .05
d. none of the above

47. Determining what constitutes chance versus non-chance results under the assumption that the null hypothesis is true is done with reference to a probability value known as a(n):
a. conditional probability
b. beta level
c. binomial probability
*d. alpha level

48. The binomial and normal distributions are closely related, with the correspondence between them depending on the values of :
*a. *n* and *p*
b. *a* and *b*
c. alpha and beta
d. the mean and standard deviation

49. The correspondence between the binomial and normal distributions:
a. improves as *p* becomes closer to .50
b. improves as *p* becomes closer to .05
c. improves as *n* increases
*d. a and c

50. For small *n*, the correction for _____ yields even better correspondence between the binomial and normal distributions.
   a. attenuation   c. small sample sizes
  *b. continuity   d. error

Chapter 7: Estimation and Sampling Distributions

Comments to Instructors

This chapter is one of the most important in the book and I warn my students that it requires abstract thinking. I tell them that it is absolutely critical that they learn this material. If they get lost here, they are doomed to failure in the class.

One common error that students make in this chapter is to assume that an unbiased estimator is one that has no sampling error. I stress to students that just because an estimator is unbiased does not mean it will accurately reflect the population parameter in any given sample. The term "unbiased" is a technical, statistical term and refers to a specific statistical property: the mean of the estimator across all possible random samples of a given size will equal the value of the population parameter. This needs to be emphasized.

The notion of a sampling distribution is an abstract concept and some students have difficulty with it. I spend extra time on this, making sure that students have a good feel for what a sampling distribution is.

At this point, it is important that the student keep in mind the distinction between populations, samples, and sample estimates of population parameters. I also emphasize this point very strongly and highlight the table on page 186 of the main text.

Examples for Class

A wide range of examples are possible for this chapter. I take the strategy of describing a set of population scores with a known mean and variance and then state that these parameter values are unknown to me. My task is to figure out what these values might be, based on sample data that I collect. I use an example where I say I want to know what the mean and standard deviation is of the intelligence of students who attend my university (SUNY Albany). In principle, I could administer an intelligence test (such as the Wechsler) to all students and then compute the mean and standard deviation. However, this is impractical, so I resort to a random sample. It is within this context that I then develop the ideas of Chapter 7.

Answers to Selected Exercises

7. variance = .75
   variance estimate = .80
   standard deviation = .866
   standard deviation estimate = .894

22. $\overline{X}$ = 5.0; estimated standard error of the mean = .224

Test Questions

1. Which of the following situations is most likely to produce a random sample?
a. a selection procedure that reduces the chances of selecting improbable events
b. balancing the sample with both improbable and probable elements of the population
*c. a selection procedure devised so that each element in the population is equally likely to be selected
d. all of the above

2. When attempting to estimate a population parameter from a small sample, _____ occurs.
a. experimenter bias
b. distribution error
*c. sampling error
d. no error

3. Estimating population parameters can be accomplished with reference to _____ populations.
a. small
b. large
c. infinite
*d. all of the above

4. The fact that a sample statistic may not equal the value of its corresponding population parameter is said to be the result of:

*a. sampling error
c. systematic error
b. random error
d. parametric error

5. The term "sampling error" reflects the fact that sample values are likely to differ from population values because:
a. mistakes have been made in the collection and analysis of the data
*b. they are based on only a portion of the overall population
c. bias has contaminated the variance estimates
d. all of the above

6. The amount of sampling error can be represented as the difference between the value of a _____ and the value of the corresponding _____.
a. standard deviation; variance
*b. sample statistic; population parameter
c. sample; population
d. mean; standard deviation

7. In practice, it is _____ to compute the exact amount of sampling error that occurs.
a. unnecessary
*c. impossible
b. difficult
d. relatively easy

8. In the absence of any other information, the _____ is your best guess about the population mean.
a. sample mean with N-1 in the denominator
*b. sample mean
c. sample mean with a correction factor in the numerator

9. If you selected every possible random sample of size N from some population, then the *average* (i.e., mean) of the sample means will be _____.
a. zero
*b. equal to μ
c. less than μ
d. more than μ

10. Which of the following is an unbiased estimator of it's corresponding population parameter?
*a. $\overline{X}$
b. s^2

11. In the absence of any other information, the sample mean that one observes is _____ of the value of the population mean.
a. a biased estimator
b. an underestimation
c. a conservative estimate
*d. one's "best guess"

12. In statistical terms, the sample mean is said to be a(n) _____ of the population mean.
a. biased estimator
*b. unbiased estimator
c. standard estimator
d. underestimate

13. An unbiased estimator of a population parameter is one whose average (mean) over all possible random samples of a given size equals the value of the:
a. sample mean
b. standard deviation
*c. parameter in question
d. statistic

14. Statisticians have determined that the sample variance is a(n) _____ estimator of the population variance in that it _____ the population variance across all possible random samples of a given size.
a. unbiased; accurately estimates
b. unbiased; overestimates
c. biased; overestimates
*d. biased; underestimates

15. An unbiased estimator of the population variance can be obtained from sample data by dividing the sum of squares by:
a. N
*b. N - 1
c. N - 2
d. none of the above

16. Which of the following is an unbiased estimator of the population variance:
a. SS/N
*b. SS/N - 1
c. (SS - 1)/N
d. $\sum(\overline{X} - \mu)$

17. Your best guess of the true population variance is the ___.
a. sample variance
b. SS/N
*c. variance estimate
d. $\sqrt{s^2}$

18. The sample variance, on average, ____ the true population variance.
a. always equals
b. overestimates
*c. underestimates
d. none of the above

19. To correct for the discrepancy between the sample variance (s^2) and the population variance (σ^2) we divide SS by ____.
*a. N - 1
b. N
c. N - 2
d. $\sqrt{N} - 1$

20. A(n) ____ of a population parameter is one whose average over all possible random samples of a given size equals the value of the parameter.
a. estimator
*b. unbiased estimator
c. biased estimator

21. Calculate the unbiased estimate of the population mean from the following sample data: 4, 5, 4, 3, 2.
a. 3.5
b. 18/N - 1
*c. 3.6
d. 5.2

22. Calculate the unbiased estimate of the population variance using the following sample data: 2, 3, 4, 5, 5.
a. 1.360
b. 1.304
c. 1.166
*d. 1.700

23. Which of the following values is the best estimate of the population mean using the following sample data: 4, 4, 4, 5, 5?
*a. 4.40
b. 4.4/N - 1
c. 3.5
d. 22/N - 1

24. The symbols for the sample variance and population variance are ____ and ____, respectively.
a. σ; σ^2
b. s^2; s^2
c. σ; s^2
*d. s^2; σ^2

25. If you were provided a set of 8 scores, ____ would correspond to the degrees of freedom associated with the sum of squares of the 8 scores.
*a. 7
b. 8
c. 6
d. none of the above

26. In statistics, the phrase ____ is used to indicate the number of pieces of information that are "free of each other" in the sense that they cannot be deduced from one another.
*a. degrees of freedom
b. degrees of deduction
c. degrees of independence
d. degrees of information

27. A sum of squares around a sample mean will always have ____ degrees of freedom associated with it.
a. several
b. N
c. 2
*d. N - 1

28. The statistical phrase "degrees of freedom" denotes ____.
a. the number of related pieces of information
*b. the number of independent pieces of information

29. In general, estimation of a population parameter becomes more accurate as ____.
*a. df of the sample increases
c. population size increases
b. df of the sample decreases
d. none of the above

30. As the degrees of freedom associated with an estimate ____, the accuracy of the estimate tends to ____.
a. increase; decrease
b. decrease; increase
*c. increase; increase
d. decrease; stay the same

31. Technically, the accuracy of a variance estimate is not a function of the ____, but rather is a function of the ____.
a. degrees of freedom; sample size
*b. sample size; degrees of freedom
c. degrees of freedom; standard error
d. sample size; population size

32. Irrespective of its specific computation, any sum of squares divided by its associated degrees of freedom is referred to as a:
a. variance estimate
b. standard deviation estimate
c. mean square
*d. a and c

33. A _____ can be formally defined as a theoretical distribution consisting of the mean scores for all possible random samples of a given size that could be drawn from a population.
*a. sampling distribution of the mean
b. sampling distribution of the sample
c. sampling distribution of the scores
d. none of the above

34. Perspectives on the mean and standard deviation of a sampling distribution of the mean, as well as its shape, are derived from an important formulation called the:
a. central tendency theorem   b. central distribution theorem
*c. central limit theorem   d. central estimate theorem

35. One result of the central limit theorem is that the _____ of a sampling distribution of the mean is always equal to the _____.
a. mean; sample mean
b. standard error; population variance
c. standard error; population mean
*d. mean; population mean

36. The standard deviation of a sampling distribution of the mean is called the:
a. standard deviation estimate   *b. standard error of the mean
c. sum of squared errors   d. none of the above

37. A theoretical distribution consisting of the mean scores of all possible random samples of a given size that could be drawn from a population is called the _____.
a. variance estimate
b. population
*c. sampling distribution of the mean
d. the central limit theorem

38. The sampling distribution of the mean can be generated by drawing random samples of _____ and forming a frequency distribution of all means.
a. different sizes   c. increasingly larger sizes
*b. the same size   d. none of the above

39. The standard error of the mean reflects the accuracy with which _____ estimate a _____.
*a. sample means; population mean
b. sample variances; population variance
c. samples; population
d. standard deviations; standard error

40. If the standard error of the mean is small, then all the sample means based on a given sample size (N) will tend to be _____ and all will tend to be _____ the population mean.
a. small; equal to
*b. similar; close to
c. dissimilar; far away from
d. large; equal to

41. Two factors influence the size of the standard error of the mean: the _____ and the _____.
a. sample standard deviation; sample variance
b. population size; variability of scores in the population
*c. sample size; variability of scores in the population
d. sum of squares; error variance

42. As the sample size increases, the standard error of the mean _____, other things being equal.
a. remains constant
b. fluctuates
c. increases
*d. decreases

43. As the variability of scores in the population decreases, the standard error of the mean _____, other things being equal.
a. remains constant
b. fluctuates
c. increases
*d. decreases

44. An implication of the central limit theorem is that the sampling distribution of the mean can be approximated by a _____ distribution when the sample size is sufficiently _____.
*a. normal; large
b. normal; small
c. binomial; small
d. binomial; large

45. When the sample size is greater than around 40, the normal approximation of the sampling distribution of the mean is:
a. biased
*b. quite good
c. positively skewed
d. variable

46. The sampling distribution of the mean can be approximated with a normal distribution given a sufficiently large sample size, regardless of the shape of the:
*a. underlying population
b. underlying sample
c. normal distribution
d. sampling distribution

47. According to the central limit theorem, the mean of the sampling distribution ____ the mean of the population.
a. is somewhat less than
b. is slightly greater than
c. greatly underestimates
*d. is always equal to

48. The central limit theorem states that a sampling distribution of the mean for a population will approximate that of a normal distribution as ____.
a. the shape of the distribution becomes more bell-shaped
*b. sample size increases
c. sample size decreases
d. skewness decreases

49. The formula for calculating the standard deviation of a sampling distribution of the mean is ____.
a. SS/N - 1
b. σ^2/N
*c. $\sigma/\sqrt{N}$
d. $\sigma^2/\sqrt{N} - 1$

50. The variability of a sampling distribution is measured by the ____.
*a. standard error of the mean
b. population variance
c. standard deviation estimate
d. sample variance estimate

51. The mean square is computed as ____.
*a. SS/df
b. variance estimate/N - 1
c. both a and b
d. MS/N - 1

52. Given: $\mu = 3.5$, $\sigma = 2.09$. Calculate $\sigma_{\bar{x}}$ for sample size of 16.
a. 7.656   b. .131   *c. .5225   d. .539

53. The standard error of the mean can be reduced by ___.
a. increasing sample size
b. reducing σ
*c. both a and b

54. To estimate the standard error of the mean we use___.
a. s   b. $s^2/\sqrt{N}$ c. $s/\sqrt{N}$ *d. none of the above

55. For the following scores, what is the estimated standard error of the mean: 3, 4, 5, 6, 6, 6, 7, 8, 9
*a. .62   b. .21   c. .59   d. .20

56. If you were to select a sample size that included the entire set of population scores, then the standard deviation of the sampling distribution based on that N would always equal ___.
a. 1.00   b. σ *c. 0   d. σ^2

57. Given the same population, the sampling distribution of the mean will show _____ than either the sampling distribution of the median or the sampling distribution of the mode.
a. greater accuracy   b. greater variability
c. less accuracy   *d. less variability

Chapter 8: Hypothesis Testing: Inferences About a Single Mean

Comments to Instructors

Like Chapter 7, I tell my students that this chapter is one of the most important in the book. The chapter builds extensively on the material in Chapters 4 and 7. I encourage students to review these chapters and make sure that they are fluent with the use of terms and materials from these chapters before undertaking this one.

A substantial portion of this chapter is learning a new vocabulary and keeping all the definitions straight. Many new terms are introduced and students must keep distinctions between them clear. There is a tendency for students to focus on successfully performing the calculations required by the one sample t test (or z test), losing sight of the bigger picture and what is going on conceptually. The result is that the student can calculate all of the right answers, but really does not know why he or she is doing the calculations and to what end. Warn the students of this tendency. The concepts and logic from this chapter will be applied over and over again in later chapters, so it is important not to emphasize calculations over concepts.

Examples for Class

For the one sample z test, I use an example of an organizational psychologist who is studying absenteeism for people in high pressure jobs. He studies absenteeism in health professionals who treat HIV infected individuals. The national average for non-vacation missed days of work is 10.5 with a standard deviation of 7. A sample of 100 health professionals who treat HIV infected individuals is sampled and records show that the mean number of non-vacation days of work missed for such employees is 12.5. The standard error of the mean is .70 and the z value is 2.86, which is statistically significant.

For the one sample t test, I use an example about the study habits of full time students at a university. There is an informal rule of thumb that each credit hour for a course requires a minimum of one hour of outside class study per week. Most students take 5 courses per semester (3 credit hours each), so students should study at least 15 hours per week outside of class. My null hypothesis is that the mean number of hours studied per week is 15 and the alternative hypothesis is that it is not equal to 15. I conduct a non-directional test on a sample of 10 students. Here is the data based on self reports of estimated study time per week:

Number of Hours
  Studied

13   18
14   17
15   19
16   16
17   15

The mean is 16, the estimated standard deviation is 1.826, the estimated standard error of the mean is .577, the t is 1.73 with 9 degrees of freedom and it is not statistically significant. The 95% confidence intervals are -.306 to 2.306 and the 99% confidence intervals are -.876 to 2.876.

Answers to Selected Exercises

6. $z = -20.143$

7. z observed = -20.143 z critical = -1.96

20. t observed = 5.595 t critical = 2.045

25. 95% CI = 74.4 + (±1.96) (7/13) = 73.345 to 75.455
    99% CI = 74.4 + (±2.575) (7/13) = 73.013 to 75.786

38. a

44. ΣX = -20.0 $\bar{X}$ = -2.0   ΣX² = 648
    SS = 608.0 $\hat{s}^2$ = 67.556 $\hat{s}$ = 8.219
    $\hat{s}_{\bar{X}}$ = 2.599   df = 9
    t observed = -.770   t critical = ±2.262
    95% CI: .-7.880 to 3.880

45. ΣX = 216.0 $\bar{X}$ = 13.50   ΣX² = 2966.0
    SS = 50.0 $\hat{s}^2$ = 3.33 $\hat{s}$ = 1.826
    $\hat{s}_{\bar{X}}$ = .4565   df = 15
    t observed = 3.29   t critical = ±2.131
    95% CI: 12.527 to 14.473

46. ΣX = .282 $\bar{X}$ = 0.01659   ΣX² = .012888
    SS = .00821 $\hat{s}^2$ = 0.000513 $\hat{s}$ = 0.022652
    $\hat{s}_{\bar{X}}$ = .00549   df = 16
    t observed = 3.019   t critical = ±2.120
    95% CI: .00494 to .02824

Test Questions

1. If the observed and expected results of some experiment are not identical, then the null hypothesis (no differences) should be _____.
a. rejected
*b. rejected only if the discrepancy cannot be attributed to chance
c. accepted
d. accepted only if experiment is repeated

2. If you conducted an experiment and observed results that indicated a very large discrepancy between the observed and expected results, then you probably would _____.
a. accept the null hypothesis of "no difference"
b. repeat the experiment until expected results are obtained
*c. reject the null hypothesis
d. repeat the experiment until no discrepancies are observed

3. Which of the following describes a typical null hypothesis?
*a. μ=150   c. μ<150
b. μ≠150   d. μ>150

4. As part of the process of hypothesis testing, the task of a researcher is to choose between _____.
a. N or n
b. Z or μ
*c. H_0 and H_1
d. μ or σ

5. If a researcher sets a critical z value equal to ±1.96, then test statistics falling beyond that range _____.
a. suggest the null hypothesis is true
b. suggest that the alternative hypothesis is false
c. indicate an error has been made
*d. suggest that the alternative hypothesis is true

6. In the process of hypothesis testing, the investigator begins by stating a proposal, or hypothesis, that is assumed to be:
*a. true
b. false
c. neutral
d. unbiased

7. If the observed result of an investigation is so discrepant from the expected result that the difference cannot be attributed to chance, then the _____ hypothesis is _____.
a. alternative; rejected
*b. null; rejected
c. alternative; accepted
d. null; accepted

8. Informally, the _____ hypothesis can be thought of as the hypothesis of _____.
a. alternative; minimal difference
b. null; significant difference
*c. null; no difference
d. alternative; mean difference

9. The set of all standard scores that are more extreme than the critical values (that is, less than the negative critical value or greater than the positive critical value) is called a(n) _____ region and constitutes a(n) _____ result.
a. acceptance; unexpected
b. acceptance; expected
c. rejection; expected
*d. rejection; unexpected

78

10. The fourth step in the one sample z test is the conversion of the observed sample mean into a z value to determine how many _____ it is away from _____, assuming the null hypothesis is true.
a. standard scores; σ
c. standard deviations; z
*b. standard errors; μ

11. The formula that we use to test the hypothesis that a simple mean was drawn from a population with $\mu=100$ and $\sigma=9$ is _____.
a. $z=(\overline{X}-\mu)/N$
c. $z=(\overline{X}-\mu)/\sqrt{N}$
*b. $z=(\overline{X}-\mu)/\sigma_{\overline{X}}$
d. none of the above

12. A sampling distribution of means based on all possible random samples of size 25, drawn from a population with a mean of 100, will have a standard error of _____.
a. 5
c. 20
b. 4
*d. can't determine above

13. A sampling distribution of means based on all possible random samples of N=25, drawn from a population having a μ of 25 and a σ of 4, will have a mean of _____ and standard deviation of _____.
a. 25;4
c. 25; .16
*b. 25; .8
d. unknown; .8

14. The formula for determining the standard error of the population mean is _____.
*a. $\sigma/\sqrt{N}$
c. $\sigma/N-1$
b. σ/N
d. $s/N-1$

15. The most likely conclusion to make if your observed z exceeds the critical value is the _____.
a. null hypothesis is true
b. the population mean is equal to the value specified in the null hypothesis
c. the sample mean is different from the population mean
*d. the population mean is different from the value specified in the null hypothesis

16. A probability value that defines a region associated with unexpected results is known as _____.
*a. alpha
b. beta
c. gamma
d. 1-alpha

17. Traditionally, _____ is the probability associated with alpha.
*a. .05
b. .025
c. .50
d. 1-.05

18. The statement "to fail to reject the null hypothesis" would be made when the observed value of z _____.
*a. falls within the region bounded by the critical values
b. falls beyond the critical values
c. could have occurred by chance less than .05
d. is -2.00

19. Rejection regions are determined with reference to a probability value known as a(n):
*a. alpha level
b. beta level
c. probability level
d. z level

20. When the alpha level is .05, a result is defined as being "unexpected" if the probability of obtaining that result, assuming the null hypothesis is true, is:
a. less than .95
b. greater than .95
*c. less than .05
d. greater than .05

21. For an alpha level of .05, an unexpected result in the one sample z test includes any sample mean occurring more than _____ standard errors below or more than _____ standard errors above the value of μ represented in the null hypothesis.
a. .95
*b. 1.96
c. .05
d. 1.0

22. When a researcher obtains a result that is consistent with the null hypothesis, he or she _____ the null hypothesis.
a. rejects
b. accepts
c. fails to accept
*d. fails to reject

23. In principle, we can _____ accept the null hypothesis as being _____ via our statistical methods.
a. sometimes; true
b. never; false
c. always; true
*d. never; true

24. When the observed value of z falls within the range defined by the critical values, we _____ the null hypothesis.
*a. fail to reject
b. fail to accept
c. reject
d. accept

25. Rejection of the null hypothesis when it is true is called a:
*a. Type I error
b. Type II error
c. Type III error
d. none of the above

26. Failure to reject the null hypothesis when it is false is called a:
a. Type I error
*b. Type II error
c. Type III error
d. none of the above

27. The probability of making a Type I error is equal to:
a. the alpha level
b. .05, in most cases
c. α
*d. all of the above

28. The probability of making a _____ error is traditionally called beta.
a. sampling
b. Type I
*c. Type II
d. rejection

29. The probability, given a true null hypothesis, of *not* making a Type I error--that is, of failing to reject a false null hypothesis--is defined by:
*a. $1 - \alpha$
b. $1 - \beta$
c. $1 - .95$
d. $1 - z$

30. The probability that an investigator will correctly reject the null hypothesis when it is false is called the _____ of the statistical test.
a. beta
*b. power
c. alpha
d. p value

31. The alpha level directly affects the power of the statistical test, with more _____ alpha levels yielding _____ tests, everything else being equal.
a. conservative; more powerful
b. liberal; less powerful
*c. conservative; less powerful
d. none of the above

32. The _____ the sample size, the _____ the statistical test will be, everything else being equal.
a. smaller; more powerful
b. smaller; less powerful
c. larger; more powerful
*d. b and c

33. As a rough guide, investigators generally attempt to achieve statistical power (the probability of correctly rejecting the null hypothesis when it is false) in the range of _____ to _____.
a. α to β
b. 0 to 1.0
c. .05 to .95
*d. .80 to .95

34. Type I errors occur when we _____.
*a. reject a null hypothesis that is true
b. accept a null hypothesis that is false
c. fail to reject a null hypothesis that is false
d. accept an alternative hypothesis only 95% of the time.

35. If a researcher rejects a null hypothesis that is true, then a _____ has been made.
a. Type II error
b. sampling error
*c. Type I error
d. correct decision

36. The probability for Type I error is equal to _____.
a. .05
b. β
*c. α
d. 1-α

37. If you fail to reject the H_0 when H_0 is false then you made a _____ with a probability equal to _____.
a. Type I error; α
*b. Type II error; β
c. Type I error; β
d. Type II error, α

38. Type II errors are made when you ____ H_0 and H_0 is ____.
a. reject; false
*b. fail to reject; false
c. accept; true
d. fail to reject; true

39. Type II errors have a probability of occurring equal to ____.
*a. β
b. 1-β
c. 1-α
d. α

40. To avoid making a Type I error, we should use ____ level.
a. a liberal β
*b. a conservative α
c. a smaller N
d. a liberal α

41. The power of a statistical test can be increased by ____.
a. increasing α level
b. increasing sample size
*c. all of the above

42. Which of the following statements is an example of a two-tailed alternative hypothesis?
a. $H_1:\mu_1>\mu_2$
b. $H_1:\mu_1= \mu_2$
c. $H_1:\mu_2>\mu_1$
*d. $H_1:\mu_1 \neq \mu_2$

43. When there is exclusive concern that the population mean differs from a value in a specified direction, we should use ____.
a. a nondirectional test
*b. a directional test
c. a stringent α
d. both a and c above

44. Which characteristics of the *t* distribution influences its shape?
a. population mean
*b. sample size
c. sample mean
d. size of confidence interval

45. The critical *t* value needed to reject the null will always be ____ than a Z value for the same set of scores.
a. less
*b. larger
c. equal
d. different

46. The terms "statistically significant" and "statistically nonsignificant" are meant to apply:
*a. only to the statistical outcome
b. only to the practical implications
c. only to Type II outcomes
d. only to real-world outcomes

47. An alternative hypothesis that specifies that a population mean is different from a given value and also indicates the direction of that difference is called a:
a. differential alternative hypothesis
*b. directional alternative hypothesis
c. a and b
d. neither a nor b

48. Directional tests are often referred to as :
a. unbiased tests
b. single distribution tests
c. one-sample tests
*d. one-tailed tests

49. In general, a directional test will be _____ than a corresponding nondirectional test if the actual population mean and the hypothesized population mean differ in the specified direction.
a. less accurate
b. less powerful
c. more practical
*d. more powerful

50. When _____, and the raw scores in the population are normally distributed, then the normal and t distributions are quite _____ one another.
a. $N < 40$; similar to
*b. $N > 40$; similar to
c. $N = 40$; different from
d. none of the above

51. A t value is analogous to a z score except that it represents the number of _____ a sample mean is from μ.
a. standard errors
b. standard deviations
*c. estimated standard errors
d. estimated standard deviations

52. The one-sample *t* test is based on the assumption that:
a. the sample is independently and randomly selected from the population of interest
b. the scores on the variable are normally distributed
c. the variable being studied is qualitative in nature
*d. a and b

53. When we say that a test is _____ to violations of a distributional assumption, we mean that the frequency of Type I and Type II errors, and, thus, the accuracy of our conclusions, are relatively unaffected as compared to when the assumption is met.
a. vulnerable   c. immune
b. sensitive   *d. robust

54. The values that define the boundaries of the _____ are called the _____.
*a. confidence interval; confidence limits
b. confidence limits; confidence intervals
c. confidence interval; alphas
d. none of the above

55. A confidence claim reflects a _____ of an extended number of confidence intervals across all possible random samples of a given size.
a. short-term performance
*b. long-term performance
c. zero-sum performance
d. proportional performance

Chapter 9: Research Design and Statistical Preliminaries for Analyzing Bivariate Relationship

Comments to Instructors

Most students readily understand the concept of a confounding variable, but they tend to have a more difficult time with the concept of a disturbance variable. I spend extra time on how and why disturbance variables are important to control. I also emphasize how important the distinction between between-subjects and within-subjects variables is because it influences the choice of a statistical test in future chapters.

Examples for Class

There are no numerical examples in this chapter. The book by Huck and Sandler (1979) cited in the main textbook is a wonderful source of material for examples that illustrate confounding variables.

Answers to Selected Exercises

4. Experimental research strategy

5. Observational research strategy

7. #2--no control group
    #3--the control group solved problems with no background noise
    #4--the control group solved math problems alone
    #5--no control group

Test Questions

1. An experimental strategy is a set of procedures which creates different values of ____.
   a. the dependent variable
   *c. the independent variables
   b. the control variables
   d. random variables

2. If a researcher administers either 0 mg, 10 mg, or 20 mg of a drug to subjects in an experiment, then the group of subjects receiving the 0 mg treatment is best thought of as a(n) ____.
   a. experimental group
   c. treatment group
   *b. control group
   d. unobtrusive group

3. Which of the following variables would be an observed variable in all research strategies?
   *a. dependent
   c. constant
   b. independent
   d. all of the above

4. If a researcher randomly places subjects in either a high, medium, or no stress condition, then the control condition is ____.
   a. not present in that experiment
   *b. the no stress condition
   c. a comparison of high to medium condition
   d. a baseline taken from either high or medium conditions

5. An ____ strategy is one where a set of procedures or manipulations is performed in order to create different values of the independent variable for the research participants.
   a. observational
   c. correlational
   *b. experimental
   d. a and b

6. The advantage of including a control group when utilizing an experimental strategy is that it provides a ____ for evaluating the effects of the experimental manipulation.
   a. statistical procedure
   c. manipulation check
   *b. baseline
   d. all of the above

7. In contrast to a(n) _____ strategy, an _____ strategy does not involve the process of actively creating values on an independent variable, but rather involves measuring differences in values that naturally exist in the research participants.
a. correlational; experimental
b. observational; experimental
*c. experimental; observational
d. experimental; cross-sectional

8. Random assignment is feasible only when an investigator is using an _____ strategy to "create" values on a(n) _____ variable.
a. experimental; dependent
b. observational; independent
c. observational; dependent
*d. experimental; independent

9. Random assignment _____ that the research groups will not differ beforehand on the _____ variable.
*a. does not guarantee; dependent
b. does not guarantee; independent
c. guarantees; independent
d. guarantees; dependent

10. Random assignment of subjects to experimental conditions is only feasible when an investigator is using _____.
*a. an experimental strategy
b. an observational research strategy
c. both of the above

11. Which of the following factors can influence the accuracy of a sample mean as an estimate of μ?
a. size of the sample
b. variance of population scores
*c. both a and b
d. none of the above

12. A _____ variable is related to the independent variable in a manner that renders interpretation of the relationship between the dependent variable and independent variable ambiguous.
*a. confounding
b. disturbance
c. control
d. quantitative

13. If a confounding variable has been included in the design of an experiment, then interpretation of the results would be ___.
a. correct for the independent variable but not for the confounding variable
*b. ambiguous
c. partially correct
d. unaffected by the confounding variable

14. A method that may minimizes the possibility of confounding due to individual differences is ___.
*a. random assignment to treatment groups
b. random selection from the population
c. representative selection

15. A variable that influences the dependent variable but is unrelated to the independent variable is called a ___ variable.
a. discrete
b. confounding
*c. disturbance
d. relational

16. Which of the following applies to a disturbance variable?
a. it is unrelated to the independent variable.
b. it influences the dependent variable.
c. it increases sampling error.
*d. all of the above.

17. Which procedure is *not* used to control for confounding variables?
*a. random selection of subjects
b. holding a variable constant
c. matching
d. random assignment to experimental groups

18. The technique of matching to control for confounding in an experiment results in ___.
a. all groups having similar variability
b. holding variability constant across groups
*c. placing individuals with comparable values on the confounding variable in all experimental groups
d. none of the above

19. The technique of placing comparable subjects in all experimental groups in an attempt to control tor confounding variables is called ____.
a. assignment randomization
b. Holding a variable constant
*c. matching
d. blocking

20. One way an investigator can reduce sampling error is to:
a. increase the sample sizes for the various groups
b. define the groups such that the variances of scores in the populations (σ^2) will be relatively small
*c. a and b
d. neither a nor b

21. A ____ variable is one that is related to the independent variable (the presumed influence) and that affects the dependent variable (the presumed effect), rendering a relational inference between the independent variable and the dependent variable ambiguous.
a. disturbance   c. suppressor
*b. confounding   d. control

22. A ____ variable is one that is unrelated to the independent variable but that affects the dependent variable.
*a. disturbance   c. suppressor
b. confounding   d. control

23. A disturbance variable increases ____ by increasing variability ____ groups.
a. estimation; between
b. sampling error; between
c. statistical significance; within
*d. sampling error; within

24. In terms of the strategies behavioral scientists use to control for confounding and disturbance variables, _____ (is)(are) applicable to both confounding and disturbance variables, while _____ can be applied only to confounding variables.
a. random assignment and matching; holding a variable constant
b. holding a variable constant and matching; random assignment
*c. holding a variable constant; matching and random assignment
d. matching; holding a variable constant and random assignment

25. The major disadvantage of holding a variable constant is that it may restrict the _____ of the _____.
a. meaning; random selection
*b. generalizability; results
c. validity; variables
d. size; sample

26. In matching, an individual in one group is "matched" with an individual in each of the other groups such that all of these individuals have the same value on the _____ variable.
*a. confounding   c. independent
b. disturbance   d. dependent

27. Since random assignment cannot be applied to observational groups, observational independent variables will always be _____ with all other variables that are naturally related to them.
a. related   c. matched
*b. confounded   d. none of the above

28. It is entirely possible for two variables to be _____ one another, but for no _____ relationship to exist between them.
a. confounded with; moderate
b. caused by; causal
*c. related to; causal
d. matched with; linear

91

29. The ability to make a causal inference between two variables is a function of one's ____, not the ____ used to analyze the data.
*a. research design; statistical technique
b. statistical technique; research design
c. statistical technique; experiment
d. observations; variables

30. Since observational independent variables will always be confounded with all other variables that are naturally related to them, ____ are typically not possible when an observational strategy is used.
a. experimental manipulations
b. correlated observations
c. statistical analyses
*d. causal inferences

31. With a(n) ____ variable, the values of the variable are "split up" between subjects instead of occurring completely within the same individuals.
a. confounding
b. independent
*c. between-subjects
d. within-subjects

32. Between-subjects designs and within-subjects designs are both viable strategies when the ____ is ____ in nature.
a. independent variable; observational
b. dependent variable; observational
*c. independent variable; experimental
d. dependent variable; skewed

33. For many observational independent variables, only ____ designs are applicable.
*a. between-subjects
b. within-subjects
c. experimental
d. factorial

34. One advantage of the within-subjects approach is that it is more ____ in terms of ____.
a. powerful; effects
b. advanced; manipulations
*c. economical; subjects
d. efficient; randomization

35. The _____ design can offer considerably more experimental control over individual difference variables than the _____ design.
a. observational; experimental
b. factorial; experimental
c. between-subjects; within-subjects
*d. within-subjects; between-subjects

36. One potential problem with within-subjects designs is the fact that the treatment in the first condition may have _____ effects that influence performance in the second condition.
a. random					c. significant
*b. carry-over				d. independent

An investigator was interested in determining if the size of a coin influenced judgments of numerosity when people were asked to make judgments of how many coins were in a pile of coins. Fifteen subjects were asked to estimate the number of pennies in a display of 43 coins. In another condition, 15 different subjects estimated the number of dimes for the same display.

37. In the above experiment, the size of the coin is also related to its value. Value is thus a _____.
a. disturbance variable			c. matched variable
*b. confounding variable		d. none of the above

38. In the above example, the value of the coin would be classified as a _____ variable.
*a. between-subjects			c. confounded
b. within-subjects				d. disturbance

39. Which of the following *does not* apply to a within-subjects design?
a. greater economy of subjects
*b. eliminates carry-over effects
c. greater control of confounding due to individual differences

93

40. When an investigator is confident that no carry-over effects will occur, which of the following designs is generally superior?
a. matched-subjects
b. between-subjects
c. observational
*d. within-subjects

41. A matched-subjects design often has the power of a within-subjects design while avoiding the problem(s) of ___.
*a. carry-over effects
b. subject economy
c. individual differences
d. all of the above

42. Which of the following levels of measurement can be appropriately analyzed with nonparametric statistics?
a. nominal
b. interval and ratio
c. nominal and ordinal
*d. all of the above

43. The extent to which conclusions made on the basis of a statistical test are unaffected by violations of the assumptions underlying the test is called ___.
*a. robustnesss
b. significance level
c. statistical power
d. all of the above

44. Which of the following can influence a test of robustness?
a. sample size
b. degree of violation
c. form of violation
*d. all of the above

45. ___ statistics require quantitative dependent variables and are usually applied when these variables are measured on a level that at least approximates interval characteristics.
*a. parametric
b. nonparametric
c. quantitative
d. qualitative

46. ___ statistics tend to focus on medians, interquartile ranges, and ordinal level measures.
a. parametric
*b. nonparametric
c. quantitative
d. qualitative

47._____ refers to the extent to which conclusions drawn on the basis of a statistical test (for example, rejection of the null hypothesis) are unaffected by violations of the assumptions underlying the test.
a. validity
b. reliability
*c. robustness
d. none of the above

48. Two important distributional assumptions are the _____ assumption and the _____ assumption.
a. non-normality; homogeneity of variance
b. normality; heterogeneity of variance
c. equal N; parametric
*d. normality; homogeneity of variance

49. Statisticians can determine the effects of violating assumptions by using _____ or performing _____.
*a. mathematical logic; Monte Carlo studies
b. observational designs; experimental designs
c. Monte Carlo studies; one-sample t tests
d. violation estimates; factorial designs

Chapter 10: Independent Groups t Test

Comments to Instructors

This is a long chapter. I think it is important to help students keep the "big picture" in mind by emphasizing the three main questions we are addressing about a bivariate relationship: (1) is there a relationship between the variables, (2) what is the strength of the relationship, and (3) what is the nature of the relationship? Again, encourage the students not to get caught up in the computational details to the exclusion of a broader conceptual focus.

A common mistake that students make is to mix up a standard error of the difference between two independent means and the *estimated* standard error of the difference between two independent means. This distinction is important. Another common error is to misspecify the null and alternative hypotheses using sample notation rather than population notation.

Examples for Class

To develop the independent groups t test, I use an experiment in which social workers are provided with a detailed case study of a father who might be abusing his son. The materials provide a family background and describe incidents that could be interpreted as abuse. The social worker is to indicate the likelihood that abuse has taken place, using a 0 to 10 rating scale (with higher scores indicating a greater subjective likelihood of abuse). A total of 20 social workers are given scenarios. The case study read by each social worker is identical in all respects except one. For half of the social workers, the parent is identified as being African American, whereas for the other half of the social workers, the parent is identified as being Caucasian. All the social workers are Caucasian. The null hypothesis is that the ethnic group of the parent will not have an effect on the mean ratings of judged abuse likelihood. The alternative hypothesis is non-directional. Here are the data (note: I also include columns of data to parallel the development of eta squared, as described in the text):

Group	X	T	X_n	X_n^2
Black	4.00	-1.00	5.00	25.00
Black	5.00	-1.00	6.00	36.00
Black	5.00	-1.00	6.00	36.00
Black	6.00	-1.00	7.00	49.00
Black	6.00	-1.00	7.00	49.00
Black	6.00	-1.00	7.00	49.00
Black	6.00	-1.00	7.00	49.00
Black	7.00	-1.00	8.00	64.00
Black	7.00	-1.00	8.00	64.00
Black	8.00	-1.00	9.00	81.00
White	6.00	1.00	5.00	25.00
White	6.00	1.00	5.00	25.00
White	7.00	1.00	6.00	36.00
White	8.00	1.00	7.00	49.00
White	8.00	1.00	7.00	49.00
White	8.00	1.00	7.00	49.00
White	8.00	1.00	7.00	49.00
White	9.00	1.00	8.00	64.00
White	10.00	1.00	9.00	81.00
White	10.00	1.00	9.00	81.00

The t value is 3.46, with 18 degrees of freedom ($p < .05$). The standard error of the mean difference is .577. The mean, standard deviation estimates, and sum of squares for African Americans are 6.00, 1.155, and 12, respectively. The corresponding values for Caucasians are 8.0, 1.414, and 18. Eta squared is .40. The sum of squares total is 50, the sum of squares explained is 20 and the sum of squares error is 30. The grand mean is 7.00. The 95% confidence interval (for Blacks - White) is -3.213 to -0.787.

As a worked out example of the independent groups t test, I use a study that explores gender differences in the use of social support. Studies show that the use of social support has many beneficial effects in terms of psychological adjustment to stressful situations.

Some researchers have hypothesized that females will be more likely to seek out and use social support networks than males. The most common theoretical base for this hypothesis stems from socialization theory in which females are socialized to be more "other" oriented and more expressive than males. In this study, a group of 10 males and 10 females who were undergoing infertility treatment were studied. The males and females were matched on a wide range of potential confounding variables (e.g., family income, ethnicity, age). Each person completed an interview in which they rated how often they talked with each of 5 referents about their infertility on a 5 point scale ranging from 1 to 5 (with lower numbers indicating less frequent contact). The ratings were summed across the five referents, yielding a score from 5 to 25. The null hypothesis is that the population means are equal for males and females. The alternative hypothesis is non-directional. Here are the data:

Gender	Support	Gender	Support
Male	6	Female	13
Male	7	Female	14
Male	8	Female	15
Male	9	Female	16
Male	10	Female	16
Male	10	Female	16
Male	11	Female	16
Male	12	Female	17
Male	13	Female	18
Male	14	Female	19

The t value is 6.07, with 18 degrees of freedom ($p < .05$). The standard error of the mean difference is .989. The mean, standard deviation estimates, and sum of squares for males are 10.00, 1.764, and 60, respectively. The corresponding values for females are 16.00, 1.764, and 28. Eta squared is .67. The 95% confidence interval for males minus females is -8.077 to -3.922.

Answers to Selected Exercises

18. Since t observed (4.464) > t critical (2.306), reject H_0.

19. $SS_{TOTAL} = 3.50$

19. $T_A = .50$
    $T_P = -.50$

21.
Alcohol	Placebo
1.50	2.00
2.00	1.50
1.50	1.50
1.00	1.50
1.50	1.00

22. $SS_{ERROR} = 1.00$
    $SS_{EXPLAINED} = 2.50$

23. $eta^2 = .714$ $eta^2 = .714$

25. Reaction time is slower when alcohol is consumed.

27. $eta^2 = .086$, which is a weak effect

33. power = .60

35. b

51. b

54. b

56. Mean for trained group = 12.00, sd = 4.61. Mean for untrained group = 7.00, s = 4.40. Estimated standard error of difference = 1.358, df = 42; t observed = 3.682; t critical = ±2.02. 95% CI for trained - untrained: 2.257 to 7.743.

57. Mean for choice group = 185.91, sd = 17.42. Mean for no choice group = 145.64, sd = 11.35. Estimated standard error of difference = 5.766, df = 23; t observed = 6.984; t critical = ±2.069. 95% CI for choice - no choice: 28.340 to 52.199

58. Mean for Eastern group = 2.40, sd = 0.84. Mean for Western group = 5.67, sd = 1.07. Estimated standard error of difference = 0.418, df = 20; t observed = 7.814; t critical = ±2.086. 95% CI for Eastern - Western: -4.139 to -2.395

Test Questions

1. Independent-groups t tests may be used to analyze the relationship between two variables when ___.
a. the dependent variable is quantitative
b. the independent variable is between-subjects in nature
c. the independent variable has only two levels
*d. all of the above

2. Which of the following conditions would make it inappropriate to use an independent-groups t test?
a. when the independent variable is qualitative
*b. when the independent variable is within-subjects
c. when the independent variable is quantitative
d. when the dependent variable is measured on a level that approximates interval characteristics

3. When the independent variable has more than two levels which of the following statistical techniques may be used to investigate the relationship between the independent and dependent variables?
a. a one-sample t test
b. a one sample z test
c. an independent-groups t test
*d. none of the above

4. The independent groups *t* test is typically used to analyze the relationship between two variables when:
a. the independent variable is quantitative in nature and is measured on a level that at least approximates interval characteristics
b. the independent variable is *between-subjects* in nature
c. the independent variable has two and only two levels
*d. all of the above

5. In an independent groups *t* test, the null hypothesis will take the form:
a. $H_0: \mu_1 = \mu_2$
b. $H_1: \mu_1 = \mu_2$
*c. $H_0: \mu_1 = \mu_2$
d. $H_1: \mu_1 \neq \mu_2$

6. In an independent groups *t* test, the alternative hypothesis will take the form:
a. $H_0: \mu_1 = \mu_2$
b. $H_1: \mu_1 = \mu_2$
c. $H_0: \mu_1 = \mu_2$
*d. $H_1: \mu_1 \neq \mu_2$

7. The null hypothesis for an independent groups *t* test states that ____.
*a. the population mean scores for each level of the independent variable are the same
b. the two groups have different population means on the dependent variable
c. the independent and dependent variables are related
d. the population variances are the same

8. The alternative hypothesis for an independent-groups *t* test states that ____.
a. the two levels of the independent variable are essentially the same
*b. the independent and dependent variables are related
c. the independent and dependent variables are unrelated
d. the dependent variable influences the value of the independent variable

9. The mean of the sampling distribution of the difference between two independent means is ____ to the difference between the population means for the groups in question.
*a. always equal
b. sometimes equal
c. never equal
d. none of the above

10. The standard error of the difference between two independent means is influenced by ____.
a. the sample size of both groups
b. population variance of both groups
*c. both a and b
d. none of the above

11. The standard error of the difference becomes smaller as sample sizes ____ and the variability of the populations ____.

a. increase; increases
*b. increase; decreases
c. decrease; decreases
d. decrease; increases

12. If the variability of scores in the populations is held constant, then increasing sample sizes results in ____ in the standard error of the difference.
a. no change
*b. a decrease
c. an increase
d. all the above apply

13. The mean of a sampling distribution of the difference between two independent means is always equal to the:
*a. difference between the population means
b. difference between the sample means
c. standard error of estimate
d. standard error of the difference

14. The standard deviation of the sampling distribution of the difference between two independent means is called the:
a. standard error of the mean
b. standard difference of error
*c. standard error of the difference between independent means
d. none of the above

15. The standard error of the difference indicates how much _____ will occur, on the average.
*a. sampling error
b. error variance
c. population error
d. differential error

16. The size of the standard error of the difference is influenced by:
a. the sample sizes
b. the variability of scores in the population
c. a only
*d. a and b

17. The standard error of the difference becomes smaller as the sample sizes _____ and the variability of the scores in the populations _____.
a. decrease; increases
b. decrease; decreases
*c. increase; decreases
d. increase; increases

18. In practice, we typically know the values of _____, but we do not know the values of _____.
*a. n_1 and n_2; σ_1^2 and σ_2^2
b. the sample means; n_1 and n_2
c. n_1 and n_2; the sample means
d. σ_1^2 and σ_2^2; n_1 and n_2

19. According to the homogeneity of variance assumption:
a. $\sigma_1^2 + \sigma_2^2 = \sigma^2$
*b. $\sigma_1^2 = \sigma_2^2 = \sigma^2$
c. $\sigma_1^2 - \sigma_2^2 = \sigma^2$
d. $\sigma_1^2 = \sigma_2^2 + \sigma^2$

20. By pooling the variance estimates from the two populations, we increase the _____ on which the estimate of σ^2 is based and thereby obtain a better estimate.
*a. degrees of freedom
b. power
c. population size
d. standard error

21. If the sample sizes are not equal, then the pooled variance estimate should be calculated _____.
a. using the unweighted mean of the variances
*b. using a weighted mean of the variances
c. by reducing the size of one group to equal the size of the other group

22. The procedure which produces a pooled weighted estimate of the sample variances combines the individual estimates in a manner which is ____.
a. proportional to their mean difference
b. unaffected by sample size
*c. proportional to their degrees of freedom
d. proportional to the size of difference between the variance estimates

23. What assumption is made so that the pooled variance estimate can be substituted for the population variances within the standard error of the differences formula?
*a. the population variances are homogeneous.
b. the population variances are heterogeneous.
c. the sample sizes are equal.
d. the sample sizes are large.

Use the following information for questions 19-25. Summary data are provided but may be omitted if the student is expected to work out a complete solution.

A researcher wanted to determine if body temperature affected judgments of temporal duration. It was hypothesized that increasing or decreasing body temperature would have a corresponding effect on one's biological clock which, in turn, would affect the perception of time. One group of 10 subjects was subjected to 15 minutes of a cold environment while 8 other subjects received 15 minutes of a warm environment. All subjects were asked to press down on a button and hold it down until 20 seconds had elapsed. A timing device was used to measure (in seconds) how long the individual actually held the button down. The data follow:

Cold	Warm
18.66	18.67
13.66	21.75
19.66	33.47
13.51	12.54
11.58	22.19

17.16   24.65
14.12   16.69
14.83   21.17
18.59
19.30

Summary statistics for this problem:

	Cold	Warm
Mean	16.107	21.766
SS	75.416	244.850
Variance estimate	8.380	34.979
Estimated standard error of the difference		2.122
t test statistic		-2.667
Eta^2		.308

24. The degrees of freedom for the t statistic is ____.
a. 18   *c. 16
b. 2   d. none of the above

25. The numerator for an independent-groups t test performed on data in the table is ____.
*a. 5.659   b. 21.766   c. 16.107   d. 2.122

26. What is the value of the pooled variance estimate?
a. 21.679   b. 160.135   c. 2.122   *d. 20.016

27. The denominator for an independent-groups t test using the data in the table is ____.
a. 4.504   * b. 2.122   c. -5.659   d. 2.667

28. The critical t value for the "cold/warm environment" problem is ____. (Assume $a = .05$, nondirectional test, and use Appendix D.)
a. 1.746   b. 2.667   c. 2.101   *d. 2.120

29. The measure of the strength of the relationship between the independent and dependent variables in the "cold/warm environment" data is ___.
*a. $2.667^2/(2.667^2 + 16)$ c. .05
b. $2.120^2/(2.120^2 + 16)$ d. $2.667^2/2.667 + 18$

Use the following data to answer questions 26-31. Assume both groups are independent, and the alternative hypothesis is nondirectional.

Group 1   12, 14, 10, 9, 11, 13
Group 2   8, 7, 10, 11, 6, 9

Summary statistics for this problem:

Statistic	Group 1	Group 2
Mean	11.50	8.50
SS	17.50	17.50
Variance estimate	3.50	3.50

30. The pooled variance estimate is ___.
a. 17.50   c. 35.00
b. 1.08   *d. 3.50

31. The estimated standard error of the difference between two independent means is ___.
*a. 1.08   b. 3.00   c. 3.50   d. 17.50

32. The calculated t test statistic is ___.
a. 11.5 - 8.5/3.5 = .857   *c. 3.00/1.08 = 2.77
b. 8.5 - 11.5/3.5 = .857   d. 3.00/1.87 = 1.604

33. The critical t value is ___. (Use Appendix D.)
a. 2.228   c. 1.187
*b. 3.169   d. 3.055

34. The value, eta^2, may be calculated using ____.
a. $3.169^2/(3.169^2 + 10)$ c. $-.435/1$
*b. $2.777^2/(2.777^2 + 10)$ d. $2.77/12.77$

35. If the observed t value exceeds the critical t value, then the difference between the sample means is most likely ____.
a. attributable to sampling error
b. nonsignificant
*c. not attributable to sampling error
d. not very reliable

36. The set of all t values more extreme than the critical values constitutes a(n) ____ result or more formally, the ____ region.
a. expected; rejection   c. expected; acceptance
*b. unexpected; rejection   d. unexpected; acceptance

37. The degrees of freedom for the independent groups t test are equal to:
a. $n_1 - n_2 + 2$ c. $n_1 - n_2 - 2$
*b. $n_1 + n_2 - 2$ d. $n_1 + n_2 + 2$

38. The t statistic follows a t distribution when:
a. the samples are independently and randomly selected from their respective populations
b. the scores in each population are normally distributed
c. the scores in the two populations have equal variances
*d. all of the above

39. Under certain conditions, the independent groups t test is robust to violations of the ____ and ____ assumptions.
a. equal n; heterogeneity of variance
b. randomization; independence
*c. normality; homogeneity of variance
d. unequal n; normality

40. If the sample sizes in the two groups are each greater than _____ and roughly comparable, then the independent groups *t* test is robust to rather severe departures of the _____ assumption.
*a. 40; normality
b. 100; heterogeneity of variance
c. 40; probability
d. 100; unequal n

41. The independent groups *t* test is quite robust to the assumption of homogeneity of variance when the _____ are _____.
a. variances; unequal
*b. sample sizes; equal
c. sample sizes; fairly discrepant
d. means; independent

42. Which of the following assumptions applies to the independent groups *t* test?
a. The samples have been randomly drawn from their respective populations.
b. The scores in each population are normally distributed.
c. The variances of both populations are homogeneous.
*d. All of the above.

43. For the *t* test to be considered robust to violations of certain assumptions, the samples should be _____.
a. relatively large
b. approximately equal
*c. both a and b
d. none of the above

44. Which of the following indices measures the strength of the relationship between the independent and dependent variables?
a. standard error of difference
b. power
*c. eta^2
d. alpha

45. A formula used to calculate eta^2 is _____.
a. $t^2 t^2 - 1$
b. $t^2/(t^2 + df)$
c. $SS_{EXPLAINED}/SS_{TOTAL}$
*d. both b and c

46. The _____ represents the total amount of _____ that exists in the data.
a. sum of squares total; error
b. sum of squares error; variability
*c. sum of squares total; variability
d. none of the above

47. Treatment effects are defined as the difference between a given _____ and the _____.
a. grand mean; population mean
b. sample mean; population mean
*c. group mean; grand mean
d. raw score; group mean

48. Unexplained variance or error variance reflects the influence of:
a. treatment effects
b. confounding variables
c. control variables
*d. disturbance variables

49. The total variability in the dependent variable, as represented by SS_{TOTAL}, can be spilt up, or *partitioned*, into two components:
*a. $SS_{EXPLAINED} + SS_{ERROR}$
b. $SS_{UNEXPLAINED} + SS_{ERROR}$
c. $SS_{EXPLAINED} + SS_{IV}$
d. none of the above

50. Eta-squared indexes the _____ of the relationship between the independent and dependent variables since it represents the _____ of variability in the dependent variable that is associated with the independent variable.
a. direction; proportion
*b. strength; proportion
c. nature; percentage
d. significance; percentage

51. _____ represents the proportion of variability in the dependent variable that is *not* associated with the independent variable--that is, the proportion of variability that is due to disturbance variables.
a. eta-squared
b. 1.00 plus eta-squared
*c. 1.00 minus eta-squared
d. eta-squared minus 1.00

52. Typically, research in the behavioral sciences involves _____ values of eta-squared.
a. extremely large
b. somewhat large
c. moderate
*d. relatively small

53. Eta-squared is a(n) _____ estimator in that it tends to slightly _____ the strength of the relationship in the population across random samples.
a. unbiased; overestimate
b. biased; underestimate
c. unbiased; underestimate
*d. biased; overestimate

54. The calculation of eta-squared _____ when the statistical test is nonsignificant.
*a. can be useful
b. is not necessary
c. is misleading
d. is not possible

55. The nature of the relationship in the independent groups t test is determined by examining:
a. eta-squared
b. omega-squared
*c. sample means
d. population means

56. When sample sizes are small, power will tend to be __, everything else being equal.
*a. low
b. moderate
c. high
d. there is no affect

57. The power of a statistical test is influenced by _____.
a. the strength of the relationship between the two variables in population
b. the sample sizes
c. the alpha level
*d. all of the above

58. As the alpha level becomes larger, the power of a statistical test _____.
a. will decrease
*b. will increase
c. remains the same
d. may decrease

59. If a mean difference is 5, the estimated standard error of a mean difference is 4 and the critical value of t for an alpha level of 0.05 is 2, what is the 95% confidence interval for the mean difference
a. 1 to 9
b. 3 to 7
*c. -3 to 13
d. -1 to 11

60. If the 95% confidence interval of a mean difference is -1 to 3, then the null hypothesis in the analysis was rejected.
a. true
*b. false

Chapter 11: Correlated Groups t Test

Comments to Instructors

At this point, there are a large number of terms that have been introduced with the phrase "standard" in them. I again like to remind my students about the importance of keeping them all straight. Also, I emphasize that it is very important to understand the conditions where you would apply the correlated groups t test as opposed to the independent groups t test.

Examples for Class

I illustrate the use of the correlated groups t test using a pretest-posttest design, because these are so common in the behavioral sciences. After presenting the example, I discuss the importance of including control groups. The example focuses on a clinical intervention designed to reduce social phobia. Social phobia is a fear of engaging in social interactions and numerous people show intense fear in this regard. There are a range of therapies for dealing with this, including relaxation techniques (teaching people how to relax in social settings), cognitive restructuring (changing people's cognitions about the consequences of interaction), and behavioral techniques (e.g., having people interact superficially with others and then gradually build up to more meaningful interactions). A measure of social phobia ranging from 0 to 100 (with higher scores indicating greater phobia) was administered to 10 individuals who had come to an anxiety clinic for treatment. One month following a ten week clinical intervention effort, the measure was re-administered to the individuals. Here are the data (note: I present some additional statistics if you want to use the nullified scores approach):

Individual	Pretest	Postest	Difference	Individual Mean
1	90	76	14	83
2	90	78	12	84
3	91	77	14	84
4	91	79	12	85
5	92	80	12	86
6	92	78	14	85
7	93	81	12	87
8	93	79	14	86
9	94	82	12	88
10	94	80	14	87

The mean and estimated standard deviation for the pretest is 92.00 and 1.491. For the posttest, they are 79.00 and 1.826. The correlation between pretest and posttest scores is .816. The mean difference score is 13.00 and the standard deviation estimate of the difference scores is 1.054. The estimated standard error of the mean difference is .333 and the t value is 39.00, with 9 degrees of freedom. Eta squared is 0.99. The 95% CI is 12.246 to 13.754. The grand mean of all data is 85.5.

As a worked example, I use a study in which 10 students are asked to judge their own intelligence on a scale that ranges from 70 to 130, where a score of 100 is described as "about average," a score of 110 is "moderately above average," a score of 120 is "quite a bit above average," and a score of 130 is cited as "extremely above average." Similarly, scores of 90 are described as "moderately below average," 80 as "quite a bit below average," and 70 as "extremely below average." In addition to rating their own intelligence, the students are asked to rate the intelligence of their typical classmate, using the same scale. The question is whether individuals will tend to see themselves as more intelligent or less intelligent than their peers. Here are the data:

Individual	Self	Peer	Difference
1	100	100	0
2	105	100	5
3	110	105	5
4	110	100	10
5	115	100	15
6	115	90	25
7	115	105	10
8	115	105	10
9	120	105	15
10	130	105	25

The mean and estimated standard deviation for the self rating is 113.50 and 8.182. For the peer rating, they are 101.50 and 14.743. The correlation between pretest and posttest scores is .279. The mean difference score is 12.00 and the standard deviation estimate of the difference scores is 8.233. The estimated standard error of the mean difference is 2.603 and the t value is 4.61, with 9 degrees of freedom. Eta squared is 0.70. The 95% CI is 6.111 to 17.889.

Answers to Selected Exercises

13. $\hat{s}_D = 1.414$ $\hat{s}_{\bar{D}} = .632$ df = 4
    t observed = 3.165 t critical = ±2.776

14. eta^2 = .715

15. -3.75 to -.245

16. Self-esteem scores were higher at time 2 than at time 1.

26. a

30. d

37. c

42. Mean before = 5.00, ŝ = 1.56. Mean after = 7.00, ŝ = 1.70
    $\hat{S}_D$ = 2.828 $\hat{S}_{\bar{D}}$ = .894   df = 9
    t observed = -2.237   t critical = ±2.262   eta² = .36
    95% CI = -4.022 to .0222

43. Mean direct = 5.44, ŝ = 1.56. Mean flippant = 3.89, ŝ = 0.78
    $\hat{S}_D$ = 1.236 $\hat{S}_{\bar{D}}$ = .412   df = 8
    t observed = 3.776   t critical = ±2.306   eta² = .64
    95% CI = 0.600 to 2.500

44. Mean full=6.67, ŝ= 2.71. Mean not full = 6.67, ŝ =3.58
    $\hat{S}_D$ = 2.216 $\hat{S}_{\bar{D}}$ = .640   df = 11
    t observed = 0.00   t critical = ±2.201   eta² = .00
    95% CI = -1.409 to 1.409

Test Questions

1. A correlated -groups *t* test can be used to analyze the relationship between two variables when _____.
a. the independent variable has only two levels
b. the independent variable is within-subjects
c. the dependent variable is measured on a ratio level
*d. all of the above

2. Which of the following statistical tests should be used to analyze the relationship between the independent and dependent variables when the independent variable is within-subjects?
a. one-sample z test
b. independent-groups *t* test
*c. correlated-groups *t* test
d. Pearson correlation

3. If a researcher used a matched-subjects design, which of the following statistical tests should be used?
*a. correlated-groups *t* test
b. independent-groups *t* test
c. two-sample independent z test
d. Pearson correlation

4. Which of the following conditions would make it inappropriate to use a correlated-groups *t* test?
a. The dependent variable has been measured on an interval level.
*b. The dependent variable has been measured on a nominal level.
c. The independent variable has been classified as nominal.
d. The independent variable has only two levels.

5. Which of the following conditions would preclude the use of a correlated-groups design?
a. small number of subjects
*b. the experimental manipulation has known carry-over effects
c. the existence of individual differences
d. the presence of disturbance variables

6. The correlated groups *t* test is typically used to analyze the relationship between two variables when:
a. the independent variable is quantitative in nature and is measured on a level that at least approximates interval characteristics
b. the independent variable is *within-subjects* in nature
c. the independent variable has two and only two levels
*d. all of the above

7. The major difference between the correlated groups *t* test and the independent groups *t* test is that the former is used when the independent variable is _____ in nature and the latter is used when the independent variable is _____ in nature.
a. between subjects; within subjects
*b. within subjects; between subjects
c. quantitative; qualitative
d. qualitative; quantitative

8. An important advantage of the correlated groups *t* test over the independent groups *t* test relates to the control of:
a. random assignment   c. confounding variables
*b. disturbance variables   d. all of the above

9. Usually, the correlated groups t test provides a _____ test of the relationship between the independent and dependent variables than does the independent groups t test.
*a. more sensitive
b. less sensitive
c. statistically significant
d. nullified

10. Which of the following statements describes a correlated-groups t test null hypothesis?
*a. $\mu_1=\mu_2$
b. $\mu_1 \neq \mu_2$
c. $\mu=0$
d. $\mu_1>0$

11. A sampling distribution of the mean of difference scores can be defined as a _____ distribution consisting of mean difference scores across individuals for all possible random samples of a given size that could be selected from a population.
a. skewed
b. bimodal
c. normal
*d. theoretical

12. The mean of the sampling distribution of mean difference scores is equal to the _____ across individuals in the population.
a. difference scores
*b. mean difference score
c. mean
d. standard error

13. When the population means in the two conditions defining the difference scores are _____, the mean difference score across all individuals in the population will equal _____.
*a. equivalent; 0
b. nonequivalent; 0
c. equivalent; 1.0
d. none of the above

14. The standard deviation of the sampling distribution of mean difference scores is referred to as the _____ of difference scores.
a. mean difference
b. variance
*c. standard error of the mean
d. sampling error

15. In the correlated groups t test, the relevant t distribution has _____ degrees of freedom associated with it.
a. N
*b. $N-1$
c. $N-2$
d. 0

116

16. When using a correlated-groups t test design, we calculate the degrees of freedom using _____, where N= number of difference scores.
*a. N-1
b. N-2
c. n_1+n_2-2
d. n_1-2

17. If your calculated t statistic was $t(30) = 6.23$, you would most likely decide to _____.
a. accept the null
*b. reject the H_0
c. fail to reject the H_0
d. reject the H_1

Use the following information for questions 21-26.

A reading readiness test is administered to 8 matched pairs of first graders. One child of each pair had 3 years of day care experience whereas the other child had none. The results of the test are shown in the following table. (Higher scores indicate greater readiness.) Assume $\alpha=.05$, nondirectional test.

Pair	Day care	No day care
1	11	7
2	14	9
3	12	10
4	9	11
5	8	6
6	8	7
7	10	8

18. The df for this problem is _____.
a. 14
*b. 6
c. 7
d. 12

19. The critical t for this problem is _____.
*a. 2.447
b. 3.707
c. 1.943
d. 2.179

20. The calculated t for this problem is _____.
a. .97
*b. 2.65
c. .39
d. 1.88

21. The eta² for the "reading readiness" data is _____.
a. .31   b. .23   *c. .54   d. .44

22. Based on the *t* calculated for the "reading readiness" data, what conclusion should the researcher state?
a. We should fail to reject the null
*b. Day care experience is related to reading readiness.

23. The correlated-groups *t* test is robust to violations of the normality assumption if _____.
a. the data is measured on a quantitative scale
b. there are homogeneous variances in the population
c. the population of difference scores is large
*d. the sample size is relatively large

24. Which of the following assumptions may be violated if a very large sample is used?
a. the independence assumption
*b. the normality assumption
c. the assumption of random selection
d. none of the assumptions may be even slightly violated

25. When using the correlated groups *t* test, it is assumed that the _____ is normally distributed.
*a. population of difference scores
b. sample of difference scores
c. sampling error
d. all of the above

26. The correlated groups *t* test is _____ to violations of the normality assumption.
a. especially vulnerable
*b. relatively robust
c. slightly robust
d. none of the above

27. If the sample size is less than 15, the correlated groups *t* test may show inflated Type I errors for data that are:
a. normally distributed
b. cross-sectional
*c. markedly skewed
d. markedly kurtotic

28. The formula for computing eta-squared for the correlated groups *t* test is _____ that for the independent groups *t* test.
*a. the same as
b. different than

29. In the correlated groups case, eta-squared represents the proportion of variability in the dependent variable that is associated with the independent variable *after the variability due to* _____ *has been removed.*
a. correlated errors
*b. individual differences
c. all disturbance variables
d. nullified scores

30. In a correlated-groups *t* test, eta^2 represents the proportion of variability in the dependent variable that is associated with the independent variable _____.
a. before the variability due to individual differences has been removed
b. after the variability due to individual differences has been added
c. after the variance has been divided by df
*d. after variability due to individual differences has been removed

31. The variance extraction technique that creates nullified scores removes sources of variability that are due to _____.
*a. individual differences
b. confounding variables
c. the dependent variable
d. all of the above

32. If the effects of individual differences have not been removed from the raw scores, the eta^2 for the correlated-groups case would be _____ than if they have been removed, everything else being equal.
a. no different
*b. smaller
c. larger
d. equal to or smaller

33. If a correlated-groups t test found significant differences due to the independent variable, which of the following procedures would clarify the nature of the relationship?
a. removing the effects of individual differences
b. eta^2
c. the p value
*d. examination of the means of each condition

34. If we were to compute the average nullified score across conditions for each individual in a correlated groups study, we would find that every individual would have _____ average score(s).
*a. the same
b. different
c. higher
d. lower

35. A correlated groups t test is analogous to an independent groups t test with the effects of individual differences _____ the _____.
a. added to; standard error
b. extracted from; independent variable
*c. extracted from; dependent variable
d. extracted from; sample

36. The analysis of the nature of the relationship for the _____ involves examination of the mean scores for the two conditions.
a. correlated groups t test
b. independent groups t test
*c. a and b
d. neither a nor b

37. When we fail to reject the null hypothesis, the question of the nature of the relationship is:
a. meaningful
*b. not meaningful
c. statistically significant
d. addressed by eta-squared

38. An important methodological problem to consider in a correlated-groups design is _____.
a. effects of individual differences
b. the need for a larger sample compared to an independent-groups design
c. the greater power of the test produces more Type I errors
*d. carry-over effects of the independent variable

39. If the sample size of a study is small and a high value of eta squared is observed, but there is no statistically significant effect of the independent variable on the dependent variable, we may conclude that _____.
a. a mistake has been made since you can't get a strong relationship when the *t* is nonsignificant
*b. unless a larger sample is used we can't be certain about the effects of the independent variable
c. although the sample is small, the strong relationship indicates there is an effect due to the independent variable
d. the nonsignificant finding should be taken as conclusive evidence of no effect of the independent variable

40. The procedure of _____ may be used in order to evenly distribute carry-over effects across conditions.
*a. counterbalancing   c. randomization
b. countersampling   d. matching

41. A correlated groups *t* test will usually (but not always) be _____ than a corresponding independent groups *t* test.
a. less powerful   *c. more powerful
b. less conservative   d. more conservative

42. In most behavioral science research, the estimated standard error for the correlated groups *t* test is _____ than the estimated standard error for the independent groups *t* test applied to the same data.
a. more stable   c. larger
b. less biased   *d. smaller

43. Using Appendix E.1, find the sample size that is need to detect a population eta^2 of .10, with a power of .80 and α=.05, nondirectional test.
a. 87   c. 53
*b. 36   d. 23

Use the following information for Question 42-46.

An experiment was conducted in which individuals' levels of hostility were measured before and after receiving a difficult test of memory. The scores on the hostility test were measured on an interval level with larger numbers indicating greater hostility. The researcher selected a Type I error protection level of .05 and a nondirectional test.

Individual	Before	After
1	12	14
2	9	15
3	8	12
4	8	14
5	10	12
6	10	14

44. The df for this problem is _____.
*a. 5   b. 6   c. 10   d. 12

45. The calculated t for this problem is _____.
a. 2.50   *c. 5.48
b. 6.124   d. 6.25

46. Using Table D, which of the following is the critical t for this problem?
a. 3.707   c. 3.365
*b. 2.571   d. 3.143

47. Based on the summary information provided and your calculations, which decision would you make regarding the relationship between the independent and dependent variables?
a. reject the alternative   c. fail to reject the null
b. accept the null   *d. reject the null

48. What was the value of eta squared?
a. .45   c. .76
b. .53   *d. .86

49. What is the lower limit of the 95% confidence interval
*a. -5.88
b. -2.12
c. -1.78
d. -4.00

Chapter 12: One-Way Between-Subjects Analysis of Variance

Comments to Instructors

This chapter involves many computational steps and, as before, it is easy to lose the big picture of what the test is trying to accomplish. I emphasize to students the need to keep in mind the three questions that we are trying to answer, (1) is there a relationship between the independent and dependent variables (2) what is the strength of the relationship, and (3) what is the nature of the relationship. The first question is addressed by the F test, the second question by eta squared, and the third question by Tukey's HSD test. All of the computations -- the sum of squares between, the degrees of freedom between, the sum of squares within, the degrees of freedom within, the means square between and the mean square within -- are merely steps along the way to getting the F ratio used for purposes of executing the F test. Students easily become confused about all the different sum of squares and mean squares in this chapter.

Examples for Class

To develop one way analysis of variance, I use an example from organizational psychology. The issue focuses on the effects of shift type on job satisfaction. There are three shift types, (a) standard (five 8-hour days, with a two day weekend), (b) concentrated (four 10-hour days, with a three day weekend), and (c) extended (10 consecutive 8 hour days, followed by four days off). Twenty four workers are randomly assigned to one of the three conditions and job satisfaction is measured after 6 months. The job satisfaction measure ranges from 0 to 100, with higher scores indicating greater satisfaction. Here are the data (presented in a form to help the initial development of ANOVA concepts as per the textbook):

Shift	X	Group Mean	Deviation from Mean
Standard	66	69	-3
Standard	67	69	-2
Standard	68	69	-1
Standard	69	69	0
Standard	70	69	1
Standard	71	69	2
Standard	72	69	3
Concentrated	76	82	-6
Concentrated	78	82	-4
Concentrated	80	82	-2
Concentrated	82	82	0
Concentrated	84	82	2
Concentrated	86	82	4
Concentrated	88	82	6
Extended	56	62	-6
Extended	58	62	-4
Extended	60	62	-2
Extended	62	62	0
Extended	64	62	2
Extended	66	62	4
Extended	68	62	6

Source	SS	df	MS	F
Between	1442	2	721	51.5
Within	252	18	14	
Total	1694	20		

For a worked example, I use an example from health psychology that examines the possibility of a "cancer personality." Three groups of six individuals each are compared on a variety of personality characteristics. The groups are (1) people diagnosed with cancer, (2) people who have been successfully treated for cancer, and (3) prediagnosed people who do not have cancer but who are similar to people in the other groups on a wide range of demographic variables. The dependent variable is internal locus of control, which measures the extent to which people believe they can control what happens in their lives. The measure ranged from 5 to 90, with higher scores indicating greater perceived locus of control. The researcher thought that the diagnosed group would show lower levels of internal locus of control relative to the prediagnosed group and the successfully treated group. Also of interest was whether successfully treated patients would "revert to baseline" (i.e., have the same mean as the prediagnosed group). Here are the data:

Group	X
Pre	67
Pre	68
Pre	69
Pre	69
Pre	70
Pre	71
Current	27
Current	29
Current	31
Current	31
Current	33
Current	35
Treated	23
Treated	26
Treated	29
Treated	29
Treated	32
Treated	35

Source	SS	df	MS	F
Between	6096	2	3048	326.57
Within	140	15	9.33	
Total	6236	27		

Answers to Selected Exercises

14.
Source	SS	df	MS	F
Between	54.00	3	18.00	3.60
Within	100.00	20	5.00	
Total	154.00	23		

21. Here is the summary table:

Source	SS	df	MS	F
Between	48.50	3	16.167	7.821
Within	41.33	20	2.067	
Total	89.83	23		

Since F observed (7.821) > F critical (3.10), reject H_0. There is a relationship between supposed task difficulty and task performance.

22. $eta^2 = .540$

23. Table summarizing results is as follows:

Comparison	Abs Mean Diff	CD	Reject?
1 versus 2	2.00	2.32	No
1 versus 3	4.00	2.32	Yes
1 versus 4	1.66	2.32	No
2 versus 3	2.00	2.32	No
2 versus 4	0.34	2.32	No
3 versus 4	2.34	2.32	Yes

44. b

52. Mean secure = 7.00; estimated standard deviation = 2.19
    Mean avoid = 3.00; estimated standard deviation = 2.19
    Mean ambiv = 2.00; estimated standard deviation = 1.10
    n = 5 per group

Source	SS	df	MS	F
Between	84.00	2	42.00	11.667
Within	54.00	15	3.60	
Total	138.00	17		

F observed = 11.667   critical $F(2, 15) = 3.68$
$eta^2 = .609$
CD = 2.843

Tukey 95% CI for secure - avoid = 1.155 to 6.845
Tukey 95% CI for secure - ambiv = 2.155 to 7.845
Tukey 95% CI for avoid - ambiv = -1.845 to 3.845

53. Mean very low = 9.50; estimated standard deviation = 2.368
    Mean average = 12.60; estimated standard deviation = 3.438
    Mean very high = 17.70; estimated standard deviation = 2.908
    Mean very high = 24.40; estimated standard deviation = 5.060
    n = 10 per group

Source	SS	df	MS	F
Between	1272.50	3	424.17	32.95
Within	463.40	36	12.87	
Total	1735.90	39		

F observed = 32.95   critical $F(3, 36) = 2.86$
$eta^2 = .733$
CD = 4.33

Tukey 95% CI for non - mild = -7.421 to 1.221
Tukey 95% CI for non - mod = -12.521 to -3.879
Tukey 95% CI for non - high = -19.221 to -10.579
Tukey 95% CI for mild - mod = -1.221 to 7.421
Tukey 95% CI for mild - high = -9.421 to -0.779
Tukey 95% CI for mod - high = -11.021 to -2.379

54. Mean very low = 3.556; estimated standard deviation = .882
    Mean average = 3.778; estimated standard deviation = 1.093
    Mean very high = 5.222; estimated standard deviation = .833
    n = 9 per group

Source	SS	df	MS	F
Between	14.741	2	7.370	32.95
Within	21.333	24	.889	
Total	36.074	26		

F observed = 8.292   critical $F(2, 24) = 3.40$
$eta^2 = .257$
CD = 1.109

Tukey 95% CI for very low - average = -1.332 to 0.888
Tukey 95% CI for very low - very high = -2.777 to -.557
Tukey 95% CI for average - very high = -2.554 to -.334

Test Questions

1. Which of the following conditions does not suggest the use of one-way ANOVA?
a. the dependent variable is measured on at least an interval scale.
*b. there are two levels of the independent variable.
c. samples are independent and randomly selected.
d. there are unequal n's.

2. The one-way analysis of variance is typically used to analyze the relationship between two variables when:
a. the independent variable is quantitative in nature and is measured on a level that at least approximates interval characteristics
b. the independent variable is *between-subjects* in nature
c. the independent variable has three or more levels
*d. all of the above

3. One-way analysis of variance is used under the same circumstances as the independent groups t test except that:
*a. the independent variable has more than two levels
b. the independent variable is between-subjects in nature
c. the dependent variable is qualitative in nature
d. none of the above

4. In one-way analysis of variance with three groups, the alternative hypothesis is:
a. $H_1: \mu_1 = \mu_2 = \mu_3$
b. $H_1: \mu_1 \neq \mu_2 \neq \mu_3$
*c. The three population means are not all equal
d. none of the above

5. An instructor administers a moral inventory to three different college classes (labeled a, b, and c) and uses ANOVA to analyze her data. Which of the following is the null hypothesis?
a. $\mu_a = \mu_b > \mu_c$
b. $\mu_a > \mu_b > \mu_c$
*c. $\mu_a = \mu_b = \mu_c$
d. $\mu_a > \mu_b = \mu_c$

6. The more different the group means are from each other (as defined by the levels of the independent variable), the more _____ there is.
*a. between-group variability
b. within-group variability
c. error variance
d. total variability

7. Between-group variability in mean scores on the dependent variable reflects:
a. sampling error
b. the effect of the independent variable
*c. a and b
d. neither a nor b

8. Greater variability of scores within a group is indicative of greater variability of scores within the corresponding population and, thus, a greater amount of:
a. systematic variance
b. treatment variance
c. explained variance
*d. sampling error

9. _____ reflects only sampling error.
a. between-group variability
*b. within-group variability
c. total variability
d. sampling variability

10. _____ is *not* influenced by the effect of the independent variable on the dependent variable.
a. between-group variability
*b. within-group variability
c. omega squared
d. eta-squared

11. The variance ratio is represented as _____ variability divided by _____ variability.
*a. between-group; within group
b. within-group; between group
c. between-group; total
d. within-group; total

12. When the null hypothesis is true, the between-group variability reflects only:
a. treatment effects
b. explained variance
*c. sampling error
d. all of the above

13. When the null hypothesis is not true, we would expect the variance ratio, over the long run, to be:
a. nonsignificant
b. greater than 0
c. less than 1.0
*d. greater than 1.0

14. The sum of squares total reflects the total variability in the _____ across all individuals.
a. independent variable
*b. dependent variable
c. nullified scores
d. total deviation scores

15. Another name given to the sum of squares within is the sum of squares:
a. total
b. between
c. explained
*d. error

16. The _____ variability can be expressed in terms of (1) the variability between the group means and (2) the variability of deviations from the group mean.
* a. total
b. between-group
c. explained
d. within-group

17. In an ANOVA context, within-group variability reflects ___.
a. group mean differences
*b. sampling error
c. both sampling error and the effect of the independent variable
d. group mean differences and sampling error

18. The formula for df$_{WITHIN}$ is ___.
a. N - 1
b. k - N
c. k - 1
*d. N - k

19. If an ANOVA study involves 3 groups and a total of 21 subjects, df$_{BETWEEN}$ is ___ and df$_{WITHIN}$ is ___.
*a. 2; 18
b. 2; 20
c. 3; 20
d. 2; 24

20. An experimenter compares 4 groups of pain patients who are administered different medications. There are 24 patients in all. SS$_{TOTAL}$ = 230 and SS$_{BETWEEN}$ = 30. Calculate F.
a. 1.5
*b. 1.0
c. 15
d. .90

21. In ANOVA, the F test is ___.
a. one-tailed
*b. nondirectional
c. directional
d. either one-tailed or two-tailed

22. The reason mean squares rather than sum of squares are used to construct the F ratio is ___.
a. MS$_{TOTAL}$ = MS$_{BETWEEN}$ + MS$_{WITHIN}$
b. sum of squares are dependent on df
*c. because they yield an F statistic with a sampling distribution of known form
d. they are less variable than the sum of squares

23. The computational formula $\Sigma X^2 - (\Sigma X)^2/N$ is used to calculate the ___.
a. sum of squares within
*b. sums of square total
c. sum of squares between
d. pooled variance estimate

24. The variance ratio of between-group variability divided by within-group variability that is computed to test the null hypothesis does not utilize measures of ____, but rather the variance ratio is based on measures of variance, or ____.
a. averages; standard deviations
b. mean squares; sums of squares
*c. sums of squares; mean squares
d. central tendency; sums of squares

25. A mean square is simply a ____ divided by its corresponding degrees of freedom.
a. variance
*b. sum of squares
c. standard error
d. standard deviation

26. The degrees of freedom associated with the sum of squares within is equal to:
a. N
b. $N - 1$
c. $k - 1$
*d. $N - k$

27. The variance ratio, formally referred to as the F ratio, is:
*a. $MS_{BETWEEN}/MS_{WITHIN}$
b. $SS_{BETWEEN}/SS_{WITHIN}$
c. $MS_{BETWEEN}/df_{BETWEEN}$
d. $df_{BETWEEN}/df_{WITHIN}$

28. The F ratio is a ratio of:
*a. two variances
b. two standard errors
c. two sums of squares
d. two means

29. The reason why measures of mean squares rather than measures of sums of squares are used to define the F ratio is that when relevant conditions are met, measures of mean squares yield a sampling distribution that closely approximates ____, whereas measures of sums of squares do not.
a. a normal distribution
b. a binomial distribution
*c. an F distribution
d. a t distribution

30. The F distribution takes on different shapes depending on the values of ____ and ____ associated with it.
a. $MS_{BETWEEN}$; MS_{WITHIN}
b. $SS_{BETWEEN}$; SS_{WITHIN}
c. $MS_{BETWEEN}$; $df_{BETWEEN}$
*d. $df_{BETWEEN}$; df_{WITHIN}

31. In all *F* distributions, the _____ value of *F* is _____.
a. lowest; 0
b. median; 1.0
*c. a and b
d. neither a nor b

32. The sampling distribution of the *F* ratio tends to closely approximate an F distribution when:
a. the samples are independently and randomly selected from their respective populations
b. the scores in each population defined by the independent variable are normally distributed
c. the scores in each population defined by the independent variable have equal variances
*d. all of the above

33. Which of the following is not an assumption of the *F* test?
a. samples are independently and randomly selected.
*b. levels of the independent variable are quantitative.
c. populations scores for each group are normally distributed.
d. scores across populations defined by the groups have homogeneous variances.

34. Under certain conditions, the F test is robust to violations of the:
a. normality assumption
b. homogeneity of variance assumption
*c. a and b
d. neither a nor b

35. The F test is relatively robust to violations of the homogeneity of variance assumption when the population variance of one group is as much as _____ larger than the population variance of the other groups.
*a. two to three times
b. four or more times
c. ten or more times
d. none of the above

36. In one-way analysis of variance, the defining formula for eta-squared is:
a. $MS_{BETWEEN}/MS_{WITHIN}$
*b. $SS_{BETWEEN}/SS_{TOTAL}$
c. $MS_{BETWEEN}/MS_{TOTAL}$
d. $df_{BETWEEN}/df_{WITHIN}$

37. The Tukey HSD test discerns the nature of the relationship by testing a null hypothesis for:
a. the F ratio
b. the significant group means
c. the treatment effect
*d. each possible pair of group means

38. The problem with testing each pair of group means by conducting three independent groups t tests is that multiple t tests increase the probability of making a _____ for at least one of the tests beyond the probability specified by the alpha level.
a. Type II error
*b. Type I error
c. a and b
d. b only

39. The rule for choosing between two competing hypotheses for the HSD test is the following: If the absolute difference between sample means for the two groups involved in the comparison exceeds the _____, then reject the null hypothesis.
*a. critical difference
b. significant difference
c. treatment difference
d. all of the above

40. Which of the following statements is *not* true?
a. Multiple comparison procedures are used to compare all possible pairs of sample means.
*b. One should always conduct multiple comparison tests regardless of the size of F.
c. Multiple t tests are not used to examine alternate hypotheses because of alpha inflation.
d. Multiple comparison procedures vary in their statistical conservativeness.

41. Which of the following statistics is used to index the strength of a relationship in a between-subjects ANOVA?
a. $SS_{EXPLAINED}$
b. Tukey's HSD
c. critical differences
*d. eta^2

42. An investigator is studying the effect on newborns' attentional processes of women taking medication during labor. It turns out that the women who take more medication deliver in hospital A while almost all of the nonmedication subjects deliver in hospital B. Hospital in this example is a ____.
a. disturbance variable
b. constant
*c. confounding variable
d. control variable

43. Which of the following best indicates the proportion of unexplained variance in a one way between subjects ANOVA?
a. $MS_{BETWEEN}$
b. $SS_{BETWEEN}$
c. SS_{TOTAL}
*d. $1 - eta^2$

44. In writing up the statistical results of a study, which statement is most likely to appear in a research report?
a. The hypothesis was confirmed at the .01 level ($F = 7.0$).
b. $MS_{BETWEEN}$ was twice the value of MS_{WITHIN}.
*c. The strength of the relationship, as indicated by eta^2, was .44.
d. The Tukey HSD critical value was 1.36.

Use the following information for questions 26-29.

A teacher compares four different methods of giving students feedback, randomly assigning four students to each condition. Student quiz scores were as follows:

Feedback method

a	b	c	d
16	12	17	17
15	10	20	15
13	13	14	21
10	12	19	21

45. Calculate SS_{TOTAL}.
*a. 197.44
b. 947.75
c. 3504.75
d. 123.67

46. Calculate MS$_{BETWEEN}$.
a. 123.67
b. 30.92
c. 24.55
*d. 123.67

47. Calculate SS$_{WITHIN}$.
a. 2980.19
*b. 73.75
c. 197.44
d. 56149

48. Calculate the F ratio.
*a. 6.70
b. .149
c. 3.34
d. 1.68

Use the following data for questions 30-33.

Given the following incomplete ANOVA summary table:

SV	SS	df	MS	F
Between	248.55		82.85	5.81
Within		16		
Total	476.55	19		

49. What is the value of df$_{BETWEEN}$?
a. 4
b. 35
*c. 3
d. 9

50. What is the value of MS$_{WITHIN}$?
a. 228
*b. 14.25
c. 393
d. 481

51. What is the value of SS$_{WITHIN}$?
a. 393.70
b. 165.70
c. 14.25
*d. 228.00

52. What is the value of eta^2?
a. 1
b. .74
c. .17
*d. .52

53. With five subjects in a group, and given the cell means $\overline{X}_1 = 7.8$, $\overline{X}_2 = 10.8$, $\overline{X}_3 = 15.6$, and $\overline{X}_4 = 16.4$, what is Tukey's HSD critical difference (CD) value ($MS_{WITHIN} = 14.25$)?
a. 4.05
*b. 6.84
c. 11.54
d. 2.39

54. Based on the CD value calculated in Question 34, one would conclude that ___.
a. μ_4 differs from μ_1 and μ_2
b. μ_2 differs from μ_4
*c. μ_1 differs from μ_3 and μ_4
d. μ_3 differs from μ_1

55. The effect of performing multiple t tests on all pairs of groups after finding a significant F ___.
a. decreases the probability of making at least one Type I error
*b. increases the probability of making at least one Type I error

56. Relative to the Scheffè procedure, the Tukey HSD test ___.
*a. produces fewer Type II errors
b. produces more Type II errors
c. yields identical conclusions

57. If the Tukey HSD value for the critical difference is 5.00 (i.e., CD = 5.00) and the mean difference between two groups in a one way between subjects analysis of variance is 3, what is the Tukey 95% confidence interval for the mean difference?
a. -2
b. -2 to 8
*c. 2 to 8
d. 5 to 8

Chapter 13: One-Way Repeated Measures Analysis of Variance

Comments to Instructors

The computational formulas in this chapter, although straightforward, are somewhat complicated and students tend to make more computational errors in them than in other chapters throughout the book. Some students have a difficult time understanding the concept of across subject variability and how this reflects individual backgrounds. I use this example: Across-subject variability is based on a person's average score across experimental conditions, with the idea being that people with higher average scores differ in their backgrounds from people with lower average scores. Suppose you and a friend are asked to rate each of five wines on a 1 to 10 scale (with higher scores indicating a better taste) and your average rating is 8 and your friend's average rating is 2. It would seem logical to conclude that you like wine better than your friend does. This may be because your friend has not had much experience with wine (at first, wine tastes sour, but then some people acquire a taste for it), or s/he got very sick on it at sometime in the past, or s/he doesn't like alcohol in general, or any other of a host of reasons pertaining to your different backgrounds and experiences. These individual differences *are* reflected in your average ratings and are statistically controlled for in a repeated measures analysis of variance.

Examples for Class

To illustrate repeated measures ANOVA, I use the example on social phobia for the correlated groups t test (see page 111 of this manual), but I add a 6 month follow-up. Here are the data:

Individual	Pretest	1 month Posttest	6 Month Posttest
1	90	76	88
2	90	78	89
3	91	77	89
4	91	79	88
5	92	80	90
6	92	78	90
7	93	81	92
8	93	79	91
9	94	82	91
10	94	80	92

Source	SS	df	MS	F
IV	980.00	2	490.00	945.00
Error	9.33	18	.52	
Across subjects	60.67	9		
Total	1050.00	29		

The means and standard deviation estimates for the three conditions are 92.0 (1.83), 79.0 (1.49) and 90.0 (1.49).

Because ANOVA concepts are developed from other chapters, I do not complete a second worked example.

Answers to Selected Exercises

5.

Source	SS	df	MS	F
IV	40.00	2	20.00	10.00
Error	36.00	18	2.00	
Across subjects	30.00	9		
Total	106.00	29		

18. $SS_{IV} = 19.60$, $df_{IV} = 2$, $MS_{IV} = 9.80$; $SS_{ACROSS\ SUBJECTS} = 14.67$, $df_{ACROSS\ SUBJECTS} = 4$, $MS_{ACROSS\ SIBJECTS} = 3.668$; $SS_{ERROR} = 13.733$, $df_{ERROR} = 8$, $MS_{ERROR} = 1.717$. Since F observed (5.708) > F critical (4.46), reject H_0. There is a relationship between level of distraction and number of pages read.

19. $eta^2 = .588$

20. 7.4 - 6.0 = 1.4; 7.4 - 4.6 = 2.80 and 6.0 - 4.6 = 1.60. CD = 2.367

35. d

41. b

50. Mean for husband = 6.50, estimated standard deviation = 0.548
    Mean for police = 5.50, estimated standard deviation = 0.548
    Mean for parents = 3.50, estimated standard deviation = 1.643
    Mean for friend = 4.50, estimated standard deviation = 1.643

Source	SS	df	MS	F
IV	30.00	3	10.00	6.817
Error	22.00	15	1.47	
Across subjects	8.00	5		
Total	60.00	21		

    F observed = 6.817   critical $F(3, 15) = 3.29$
    $eta^2 = .577$
    CD = 2.017

    Tukey 95% CI for husband - police = -1.017 to 3.017
    Tukey 95% CI for husband - parents = 0.983 to 5.017
    Tukey 95% CI for husband - friend = -.017 to 4.017
    Tukey 95% CI for police - parents = -.017 to 4.017
    Tukey 95% CI for police - friend = -1.017 to 3.017
    Tukey 95% CI for parents - friend = -3.017 to 1.017

51. Mean for before = 212.00, est. standard deviation = 23.102
    Mean for after = 199.75, est. standard deviation = 21.644
    Mean for follow-up = 210.50, est. standard deviation = 23.046

Source	SS	df	MS	F
IV	714.33	2	357.17	29.13
Error	171.67	14	12.26	
Across subjects	10561.83	7		
Total	11447.83	23		

F observed = 29.13   critical $F(2, 14)$ = 3.74
eta^2 = .806   CD = 4.58

Tukey 95% CI for before - after = 7.670 to 16.830
Tukey 95% CI for before - follow-up = -3.080 to 6.080
Tukey 95% CI for after - follow-up = -15.330 to -6.170

52. Mean for plan = 4.57, estimated standard deviation = 0 .976
    Mean for pack = 3.86, estimated standard deviation = 0 .690
    Mean for travel = 5.86, estimated standard deviation = 0.690
    Mean for adjust = 3.57, estimated standard deviation = 0.975
    Mean for reorganize = 5.71, estimated standard deviation = 0.755

Source	SS	df	MS	F
IV	30.57	4	7.643	23.431
Error	7.83	24	.326	
Across subjects	12.74	6		
Total	51.14	34		

F observed = 6.817   critical $F(3, 15)$ = 3.29
eta^2 = .796
CD = 0.90

Tukey 95% CI for plan - pack = -0.190 to 1.610
Tukey 95% CI for plan - travel = -2.190 to -.390
Tukey 95% CI for plan - adjust = 0.100 to 1.900
Tukey 95% CI for plan - reorg = -2.04 to -.240
Tukey 95% CI for pack - travel = -2.900 to -1.100
Tukey 95% CI for pack - adjust = -0.610 to 1.190
Tukey 95% CI for pack - reorg = -2.750 to -0.950
Tukey 95% CI for travel - adjust = 1.390 to 3.190
Tukey 95% CI for travel - reorg = -0.750 to 1.050
Tukey 95% CI for adjust - reorg = -3.040 to -1.240

Test Questions

1. A one-way repeated analysis of variance is not appropriate when _____.
a. the dependent variable is quantitative and on an approximately interval scale
b. the independent variable is qualitative and a within-subjects variable
c. there are 4 levels of the independent variable
*d. the dependent variable is qualitative

2. The null hypothesis of a one-way repeated ANOVA is _____.
*a. all the population means are equal
b. all the population means are not equal
c. some of the population means are equal
d. some of the population means are not equal

3. The alternative hypothesis in a one-way repeated ANOVA is _____.
a. all the population means are equal
*b. all the population means are not equal
c. some of the population means are equal
d. some of the population means are not equal

4. The variability in the dependent variable of a one-way repeated ANOVA can be partitioned into _____ components.
a. 2
b. 4
*c. 3
d. none of the above

5. The one-way repeated measures analysis of variance is typically used to analyze the relationship between two variables when:
a. the independent variable is quantitative in nature and is measured on a level that at least approximates interval characteristics
b. the independent variable is *within-subjects* in nature
c. the independent variable has three or more levels
*d. all of the above

6. One-way repeated measures analysis of variance is an extension of the:
*a. correlated groups t test
b. independent groups t test
c. matched groups t test
d. none of the above

7. In a repeated measures design, the components comprising the total variability in the dependent variable include:
a. sum of squares IV
b. sum of squares across subjects
c. sum of squares error
*d. all of the above

8. The sum of squares IV is conceptually similar to the _____ in the between-subjects analysis of variance.
a. sum of squares within groups
*b. sum of squares between groups
c. sum of squares total
d. sum of squares error

9. The _____ is the component that differentiates the repeated measures design and the between-subjects design.
a. sum of squares within groups
b. sum of squares between groups
*c. sum of squares across subjects
d. sum of squares error

10. When a _____ design is used, it is not possible to estimate the effects of disturbance variables due to individual differences.
a. within-subjects
*b. between-subjects

11. The variability in the dependent variable of a one-way repeated ANOVA that reflects the influence of the independent variable is the _____ and is conceptually equivalent to _____ in a between-subjects design.
a. sum of squares IV; sum of squares within
*b. sum of squares IV; sum of squares between
c. sum of squares between; sum of squares error
d. sum of squares within; sum of squares error

12. The variability component in a one-way repeated ANOVA that differentiates it from the between-subjects design is the _____.
a. sum of squares IV
*c. sum of squares subjects
b. sum of squares total
d. sum of squares error

Use the summary values given here to help calculate the values called for in Questions 13-21.

$\sum X^2 = 704$ $(\sum X)^2 = 8464$ $\sum T_j^2 = 3178$
$\sum X = 92$ $k=3$ $N = 5$ $\sum s_i^2 = 1898$

13. Based on the summary values given above, what is the value of the sum of squares IV?
a. 139.73   *b. 71.33   c. 68.40   d. 2.40

14. Based on the summary values given above, what is the value of the sum of squares subjects?
a. 139.73   b. 71.33   *c. 68.40   d. 2.4

15. Based on the summary values given above, what is the value of the sum of squares total?
*a. 139.73   b. 71.93   c. 68.40   d. 2.40

16. Based on the summary values given above, what is the value of the sum of squares error?
a. 139.73   b. 70.93   c. 66.40   *d. 2.4

17. Based on summary values given above, the value of degrees of freedom associated with sum of squares total and the sum of squares error is _____ and _____, respectively.
a. 2; 4   *b. 14; 8   c. 4; 14   d. 8; 2

18. Based on the summary values given above, what is the value of the mean square error?
a. 33.2   b. 8.92   *c. 35.67   d. 4.19

19. Based on the summary values given above, what is the value of the mean square error?
a. 33.2   b. 1.2   c. 35.47   *d. 8.55

20. Based on the summary values given above and your responses to Questions 13-19, what is the value of F?
*a. 4.17 b. .24 c. 27.67 d. 7.43

21. Based on the summary values given earlier, what is the value of eta^2?
*a. .51 b. .97 c. .86 d. .59

22. For an alpha level of .05, the critical value of F with 2 and 8 degrees of freedom is 4.46; therefore, we _____ the null hypothesis with an F value equal to that found in Question 20 and conclude that _____ between treatments and the dependent variable.
a. reject; no relationship exists
b. fail to reject; no relationship exists
*c. reject; a relationship exists
d. fail to reject; a relationship exists

23. If the observed value of F is _____ than the critical value of F, then the null hypothesis is rejected and we can conclude that _____ an influence of the independent variable.
*a. greater; there is   c. greater; there is not
b. less; there is not   d. less; there is

24. In the summary table of a one-way repeated ANOVA, _____ degrees of freedom values and _____ F values are recorded.
a. 3; 2   b. 2; 3   c. 4; 1   *d. 1; 4

25. The mean square error in the repeated measures case will tend to be _____ than the mean square within in the between-subjects case.
*a. smaller   c. equal to
b. larger   d. more biased

26. The function of the sum of squares subjects is to remove variability due to _____ from the dependent variable so that a more sensitive test of the relationship between the independent and dependent variables can be performed.
a. treatment effects   c. group differences
*b. individual differences   d. none of the above

27. If the null hypothesis is true, the _____ reflects only sampling error.
a. mean square error
b. mean square IV
*c. a and b
d. neither a nor b

28. The *F* test for one-way repeated measures analysis of variance is appropriate when the dependent variable is _____ in nature and measured on a level that approximates _____ level characteristics.
*a. quantitative; interval
b. quantitative; ratio
c. qualitative; nominal
d. qualitative; interval

29. The _____ assumption states that the variance of the population difference scores for any two conditions is the same as the variance of the population difference scores for any other two conditions.
a. heteroscedasticity
b. normal differences
c. homogeneity of differences
*d. sphericity

30. The *F* test is robust to violations of the _____ assumption.
a. independent sampling
b. random sampling
c. sphericity
*d. normality

31. For sample sizes larger than _____, the Type I error rate remains near the specified alpha level even in the face of marked _____.
a. 10; non-normality
*b. 30; non-normality
c. 100; sphericity
d. 30; sphericity

32. In general, the *F* test is not robust to violations of the _____ assumption.
a. normality
*b. sphericity
c. a and b
d. neither a nor b

33. Many statisticians recommend that modifications be made to the _____ unless one is confident that sphericity holds.
a. Huynh-Feldt epsilon
b. Greenhouse-Geisser epsilon
*c. traditional *F* test
d. sum of squares IV

147

34. Unless one is confident on theoretical grounds that sphericity holds, it is probably best to apply the appropriate correction to the degrees of freedom via the _____ procedure.
*a. Huynh-Feldt
b. Greenhouse-Geisser
c. Mauchly
d. modified Bonferroni

35. If the assumption of sphericity is satisfied, then the nature of the relationship following a statistically significant one-way repeated measures analysis of variance can be addressed with the _____ test.
a. Huynh-Feldt
b. modified Bonferroni
c. Mauchly
*d. Tukey HSD

36. If the assumption of sphericity is not met, then the _____ procedure is used to evaluate the nature of the relationship.
a. Huynh-Feldt
*b. modified Bonferroni
c. Mauchly
d. Tukey HS

37. An assumption of the F test is that the sample is _____ selected from the population.
a. independently
*b. independently and randomly
c. randomly

38. Violations of the assumption of _____ lead to increased _____ error.
a. normality; Type I
*b. sphericity; Type I
c. normality; Type II
d. sphericity; Type II

39. Modification of the _____ is necessary if the assumption of sphericity is violated.
a. sample size
b. sums of squares
*c. degrees of freedom
d. treatments

40. Degrees of freedom adjustment factors for violation of the sphericity assumption result in degrees of freedom for _____ that are _____ the traditional degrees of freedom.
*a. IV and error; less than or equal to
b. total and subject; less than or equal to
c. IV and error; greater than
d. total and subjects; greater than

41. Eta² reflects the proportion of variance in the dependent variable associated with the _____ after variability due to _____ has been removed.
*a. independent variable; individual differences
b. individual differences; independent variable
c. independent variable; error
d. individual differences; error

42. If the null hypothesis is rejected, the _____ procedure will allow us to examine the nature of the relationship.
*a. HSD   c. F test
b. q value   d. alpha

43. Given a q value of 4.6, N=5, MS_{ERROR} = 2.4, and condition sample means of 6.89, 11.00, and 5.2, you could conclude that _____.
*a. condition 1 has a statistically significantly higher mean than condition 2 and 3, which are not statistically significantly different from each other
b. condition 2 has a statistically significant higher mean than condition 3, but there are no other statistically significant differences
c. there are no statistically significant differences between the means of any of the conditions
d. condition 2 has a statistically significantly higher mean than condition 1, and condition 1 has a statistically significantly higher mean than condition 3

44. When comparing a between-subjects design with a repeated design, the between-subjects design will _____ powerful than the repeated design.
a. always be less   c. always be more
*b. usually be less   d. usually be more

45. The sum of squares within from a one-way between-subjects analysis of variance is mathematically equal to the total of the sum of squares _____ and the sum of squares _____ from a one-way repeated measures analysis of variance applied to the same scores.
a. IV; error   *c. subjects; error
b. subjects; IV   d. none of the above

46. The degrees of freedom for the denominator of the *F* test will always be _____ in the repeated measures case than in the between-subjects case.
*a. less
b. larger
c. more accurate
d. none of the above

47. _____ serves to turn confounding variables associated with treatment order into disturbance variables.
* a. Counterbalancing
b. Random assignment
c. Random selection
d. Sphericity

48. An alternative to counterbalancing as a means of controlling confounding variables is to _____ the conditions for each subject.
a. systematically order
*b. randomly order
c. carefully order
d. selectively order

49. Randomly ordering the conditions for each subject is particularly valuable when the number of _____ is so great that counterbalancing is impossible.
a. effects
b. variables
c. subjects
*d. conditions

50. To the extent that the dependent variable is influenced by individual background, the population eta-squared will be _____ in the within-subjects case than in the between-subjects case.
*a. greater
b. smaller
c. more interpretable
d. less interpretable

Chapter 14: Pearson Correlation and Regression: Inferential Aspects

Comments to Instructors

Most of the material in this chapter is an extension of the material in Chapter 5. I tell students to re-read and carefully study Chapter 5 before reading this chapter. Students need to have emphasized the distinction between a population regression equation and a sample regression equation. Students often fail to maintain the proper distinction, and use the two interchangeably.

Examples for Class

I use an example of the relationship between extroversion when a child is 6 years old and how extroverted the child is as a teenager. Ten children are given a measure of extroversion when they are 6 years old and again when they are 18 years old. Here are the data (measured on a scale that ranges from 0 to 15, with higher scores indicating more extroversion):

Six	Eighteen
2	1
3	5
3	4
4	5
4	0
4	1
4	5
5	12
5	6
6	9

The mean and estimated standard deviation for age 6 is 4.00 and 1.16 and for age 18 it is 4.80 and 3.71. The correlation is .65, and the regression equation for predicting extroversion at age 18 from extroversion at age 6 is Y = -3.533 + 2.083X. The estimated standard error of estimate is 2.99. The 95% confidence interval for the correlation is 0.034 to 0.908. This is a good example to illustrate prediction and regression for purposes of forecasting how extroverted someone will be based on their early childhood extroversion. I discuss if the data from person 8 could be an outlier.

Another example I use is based on a test-retest reliability analysis of an acculturation scale (i.e., how acculturated Hispanic immigrants become to the U.S. culture, with higher scores indicating greater degrees of acculturation). I use this as an opportunity to teach students a little about psychometrics. I describe a test-retest study with a three week interval between testing periods. The scale ranges from 0 to 100, with higher scores indicating greater acculturation. Here are the data:

Time 1	Time 2
41	38
50	57
47	54
46	38
31	43
32	35
47	42
66	65
48	56
47	54

The mean and estimated standard deviation for the time 1 data are 45.50 and 9.81. For time 2, it is 48.20 and 10.20 The correlation is .78, and the regression equation for predicting time 2 acculturation from time 1 acculturation is Y = 11.128 + .815X. The estimated standard error of estimate is 6.712. The 95% confidence interval for the correlation is 0.295 to 0.945.

Answers to Selected Exercises

10. $r = .578$
    Since r observed $(.578) > r$ critical $(.553)$, reject H_0.

11. $r^2 = .334$

12. 0.040 to 0.856

13. The two variables are positively related.

25. $\hat{Y} = 3.00 + .5775X$

    a. $\hat{Y} = 3.00 + (.5775)(2)$
   $= 3.00 + 1.16$
   $= 4.16$

    b. $\hat{Y} = 3.00 + (.5775)(8)$
   $= 3.00 + 4.62$
   $= 7.62$

    c. $\hat{Y} = 3.00 + (.5775)(8.5)$
   $= 3.00 + 4.91$
   $= 7.91$

26. estimated standard error of estimate $= 2.30$

31. b

41. b

45. d

46. b

48. $r = -.8004$
    95% CI = -0.942 to -0.419
    Since r observed (-.8004) < r critical (-.497), reject H_0.
    $\hat{Y} = 22.023 + (-.8299)X$
    estimated standard error of estimate = 2.414

49. $r = .0913$ r critical = .468
    $\hat{Y} = 78.14 + (.13)X$
    estimated standard error of estimate = 6.95

51. r observed = .8041 r critical = .532
    $\hat{Y} = 9.65 + (.89)X$
    estimated standard error of estimate = 3.87

    a. $\hat{Y} = 9.65 + (.89)(38)$
          = 9.65 + 33.82
          = 43.47   (hire)

    b. $\hat{Y} = 9.65 + (.890)(42)$
          = 9.65 + 37.38
          = 47.03   (hire)

    c. $\hat{Y} = 9.65 + (.89)(30)$
          = 9.65 + 26.70
          = 36.35   (do not hire)

    d. $\hat{Y} = 9.65 + (.89)(34)$
          = 9.65 + 30.26
          = 39.91   (do not hire)

    e. $\hat{Y} = 9.65 + (.89)(36)$
          = 9.65 + 32.04
          = 41.69   (hire)

    f. $\hat{Y} = 9.65 + (.89)(31)$
          = 9.65 + 27.59
          = 37.24   (do not hire)

g. $\hat{Y} = 9.65 + (.89)(44)$
    $= 9.65 + 39.16$
    $= 48.81$ (hire)

h. $\hat{Y} = 9.65 + (.89)(35)$
    $= 9.65 + 31.15$
    $= 40.80$ (hire)

Test Questions

1. The Pearson correlation cannot be used to determine the relationship between two variables when _____.
a. both variables are quantitative and on an interval level
b. both variables are measured on the same individuals and are on a ratio level
*c. one variable is quantitative and the other is qualitative in nature with three or more levels
d. none of these are exceptions, it can be used in all of these cases

2. The Pearson correlation is typically used to analyze the relationship between two variables when:
a. both variables are qualitative in nature
b. the two variables have been measured on different individuals
c. the observations on each variable are within-subjects in natured.
*d. none of the above

3. The general form of the linear model is:
a. $Y = \alpha + \beta X + \epsilon$ c. $\epsilon = \alpha + \beta X + Y$
b. $X = \alpha + \beta Y + \epsilon^2$ d. $Y = \beta + \alpha X + \epsilon$

4. The linear model states that a person's score on Y is a linear function of X, with α representing the _____ and β representing the _____.
a. slope; intercept   c. slope; error score
b. intercept; slope   d. error score; intercept

5. It is ____ in the behavioral sciences that a(n) ____ correlation exists between Y and X.
a. rare; imperfect
b. rare; linear
c. common; perfect
d. rare; perfect

6. In the linear model, ϵ is called an error score and reflects all factors that are ____ with X that influence Y.
a. correlated
b. uncorrelated
c. contiguous
d. associated

7. When a relationship is found using the Pearson correlation technique on sample data, this does not mean there is a non-zero correlation in the population, because of ____.
*a. sampling error
b. sample size
c. restriction of range
d. none of these, since it will always exist in the population if it is present in the sample

8. If a relationship is observed between two variables in a set of sample data, this ____ that a relationship exists in the corresponding population.
*a. does not always mean
b. always means

9. A relationship might exist in a sample even though it does not exist in the population, because of:
a. idiosyncratic variance
b. incorrect inference
c. confounding variables
*d. sampling error

10. Nonzero correlation coefficients indicate some approximation to a ____ relationship.
*a. linear
b. nonlinear
c. causal
d. bidirectional

11. The traditional null hypothesis in a Pearson correlation problem states that the ____ between two variables is 0.
a. nonlinear relationship
b. semipartial correlation
c. population correlation
d. sample correlation

12. Which of the following values represents the weakest correlation between variables?
a. +.95
b. -.60
c. +.10
*d. -.04

13. Which of the following values represents the strongest correlation between variables?
a. 0
*b. -.80
c. +.75
d. -.15

14. The traditional null hypothesis tested using the Pearson correlation is _____.
*a. the correlation in the population equals 0
b. the correlation in the population does not equal 0
c. the correlation in the population is greater than 0
d. the correlation in the population equals 1

15. The sampling distribution of the population correlation coefficient is _____ when the population coefficient is equal to 0.
a. positively skewed
b. negatively skewed
*c. symmetrical and approximately normal
d. bimodal

16. When the population correlation coefficient is greater than 0, the sampling distribution is _____.
*a. positively skewed
b. negatively skewed
c. symmetrical and approximately normal
d. bimodal

17. When testing the significance of a correlation, we use the alpha level and the degrees of freedom value equal to _____.
a. N
b. N-1
c. n
*d. N-2

18. The mean of a sampling distribution of the correlation coefficient is approximately:
a. μ, the true population mean
*b. ρ, the true population correlation
c. σ, the true population correlation
d. none of the above

19. When the population correlation is _____ and the scores in the population are (bivariate) normally distributed, then as N increases the distribution of the sample correlation coefficient tends, somewhat slowly, toward a _____.
a. 1.00; normal distribution
*b. zero; normal distribution
c. -1.00; binomial distribution
d. -1.00; normal distribution

20. We can test the null hypothesis that ρ = 0 by transforming the sample correlation coefficient into a statistic that has a sampling distribution that closely approximates the _____ distribution with _____ degrees of freedom.
a. F; $N - 1$
b. F; $N - 2$
c. t; $N - 1$
*d. t; $N - 2$

21. The test of the null hypothesis that ρ = 0 is based on the assumption that:
a. the sample is independently and randomly selected from the population of interest
b. the distribution of Y scores at any value of X is normal on the population
c. the variability of Y scores is the same at each value of X
*d. all of the above

22. The measure of the strength of the relationship found using the Pearson correlation is _____.
a. r^2
b. eta^2
c. SS_{ERROR} / SS_{TOTAL}
*d. a and b

23. The value of r^2 represents the proportion of variability _____.
*a. in the dependent variable that is associated with the independent variable
b. that is due to disturbance variables

c. that is unaccounted for

24. Which of the following is formally known as the coefficient of determination?
a. r
b. eta^2
*c. r^2
d. rho

25. The nature of the relationship in a correlation analysis is determined by examining _____.
a. r^2
*b. the sign of r
c. a Tukey HSD test
d. inspection of group means

26. If we find a high correlation between variables X and Y, we can conclude _____.
a. X causes Y
b. Y causes X
c. X and Y have the same cause
*d. X and Y systematically vary together

27. A positive correlation between height and weight would indicate that _____.
*a. the taller a person is, the more he/she is likely to weigh
b. the taller a person is, the less he/she is likely to weigh
c. height and weight have little to do with each other

28. Variance heterogeneity can be problematic for the t test of the Pearson correlation coefficient, especially if one is going to pursue estimation of the:
a. population variance   *c. population regression equation
b. sample correlation coefficient   d. population mean

29. The strength of the relationship between two variables in a correlational analysis can be represented by:
a. eta-squared   *c. eta-squared and r^2
b. r^2 d. t^2 and F^2

30. Another index of the strength of the effect that one variable has on another is the:
*a. slope
b. intercept
c. error score
d. none of the above

31. The slope indicates the number of units Y is predicted to change given a _____ in X.
a. linear change
b. zero order change
c. two unit reduction
*d. one unit change

32. The use of the slope as an index of effect size only makes sense when the correlation between Y and X is:
a. relatively low
*b. relatively high
c. 0
d. +1.00 or -1.00

33. The nature of the relationship between two correlated variables is determined through examination of the _____ of the correlation coefficient observed in the _____.
a. absolute value; population
b. strength; population
*c. sign; sample
d. squared value; sample

34. If the test of a Pearson correlation yields statistically significant results, researchers will sometimes pursue analysis of the:
*a. regression equation
b. sample means
c. group means
d. bivariate normal distribution

35. An investigation of the relationship between years of formal education and IQ that was conducted with a sample size of 100 found a statistically significant correlation of .25. Another investigation of the same relationship had the same r value based on a sample size of 10, but it was not statistically significant. Why might this be?
a. a sample size of 100 has too much sampling error
b. a sample size of 10 is more likely to produce a Type I error
*c. as sample size increases so does the power of the statistic
d. the standard error was larger in the sample where N = 100

36. In a regression equation, the variable being predicted (or ____)
is known as a(n) _____ variable.
a. X; dependent or criterion   *c. Y; dependent or criterion
b. X; independent or predictor   d. Y; independent or predictor

37. In a regression equation, the variable from which predictions are being made (or_____) is known as a(n) _____ variable.
a. X; dependent or criterion   c. Y; dependent or criterion
*b. X; independent or predictor d. Y; independent or predictor

38. Suppose research conducted at a secretarial school found that reading speed correlated highly with typing speed after training, and that the regression equation based on the data from this school took the form of Y=25+.25X. A new applicant has a reading speed of 400 words per minute. With training in typing, she will probably learn to type at the rate of _____ words per minute.
a. 100   c. 75
*b. 125   d. 150

39. If X helps to predict Y, then the estimated standard error of estimate will be _____ than the estimated standard deviation of _____.
a. larger; X   c. smaller; X
b. larger; Y   *d. smaller; Y

40. Suppose a school psychologist found a correlation between SAT scores of students who graduated from her school and their GPAs at the end of the first year in college. The correlation, r = .82, was based on a sample of 55 students whose SAT scores ranged from 450 to 550. The next year, one for her students made a 625 on the SAT and she wants to predict that students future GPA. Which of the following statements is true?
*a. her prediction may be incorrect
b. her will be prediction definitely be correct

41. The ability to make a causal inference between two variables is a function of the _____.
a. level of measurement of the variables
b. precision of measurement of the DV
*c. research design
d. statistical technique used to analyze the data

42. Fisher's transformation of r to z permits us to _____.
a. better characterize the size of the correlation
b. estimate the standard error of estimate
*c. test the null hypothesis that ρ is equal to any a priori specified value
d. use a test that makes fewer assumptions than the Pearson correlation

43. An important characteristic of regression is that _____ can be extended to individuals who were not included in the original data set.
a. correlated errors
b. missing data
c. sample means
*d. predictions

44. The values of _____ are estimates of _____, respectively.
a. α and β; a and b
*b. a and b; α and β
c. a and b; ρ and ϵ
d. σ and μ; a and b

45. In the context of regression, the variable being predicted, Y, is formally known as the *dependent* or _____ variable; the variable from which predictions are made, X, is formally known as the *independent* or _____ variable.
a. confounding; disturbance
b. exogenous; predictor
*c. criterion; predictor
d. predictor; criterion

46. The estimated standard error of the estimate is an index of how much error will occur in the population when:
*a. predicting Y from X
b. predicting ϵ
c. predicting Y from ϵ
d. predicting α from β

47. If X helps to predict Y, then the estimated _____ will be smaller than the estimated _____ of Y.
a. standard deviation; standard error of estimate
*b. standard error of estimate; standard deviation
c. standard error of estimate; slope
d. error scores; standard deviation

48. The _____ of the estimated standard error of estimate provides a measure of the amount of predictive error that occurs.
a. mean
b. standard deviation
c. relative magnitude
*d. absolute magnitude

Chapter 15: Chi Square Test

Comments to Instructors

A common source of confusion among students is the distinction between the chi square statistic and the chi square distribution. I stress the following: The chi square statistic is an index that is calculated in a set of sample data. It reflects how discrepant the observed and expected frequencies are *in the sample data*. The reason we prefer the formula we use to document discrepancies between expected and observed frequencies is because it yields a statistic that has a sampling distribution that closely approximates the theoretical chi square distribution. The theoretical chi square distribution is a distribution that we know a great deal about and we can specify probabilities of obtaining ranges of scores within it. This makes the chi square statistic a very useful index of the discrepancies between observed and expected frequencies because we can use our knowledge of the chi square distribution to make statements about the sampling distribution of the chi square statistic.

Examples for Class

To develop the logic of the chi square test, I use a 3x2 contingency table. It examines whether or not a person was abused as a child and how this is related to their marital status at age 30. Here are the data:

	Single	Married	Divorced or Separated	Total
Abused	10	20	70	100
Not Abused	90	380	430	900
Total	100	400	500	

The expected frequencies are as follows:

	Single	Married	Divorced or Separated
Abused	10	40	50
Not Abused	90	360	450

The chi square is 20.00 (df = 2) and the value of Cramer's V is .14.

A second example I use is with a 2X2 table. This example examines whether a child grew up in a household where there was at least one parent who was an alcoholic and how this related to the child ultimately attaining a college degree. The question is whether the parent's alcohol history is associated with a child's attainment of a college degree. Here are the data:

	Alcoholic	No Alcohol	Total
College Degree	40	300	340
No College Degree	160	500	660
Total	200	800	

The expected frequencies are as follows:

	Alcoholic	No Alcohol
College Degree	68	272
No College Degree	132	528

The chi square is 212.84 and the value of fourfold point correlation is .15.

Answers to Selected Exercises

17. $\chi^2 = 13.187$
    Since χ^2 observed (13.187) > χ^2 critical (9.488), reject H_0.

18. $V = .1624$

19. There are more City Republicans than expected and fewer City Democrats and Suburban Republicans than expected.

30. $\chi^2 = 11.450$
Since χ^2 observed (11.450) > χ^2 critical (5.991), reject H_0.

31. Brown eyes are over-represented and blue-eyes are under-represented in the population of interest.

39. d

47. χ^2 observed = 66.82 χ^2 critical = 5.991 $V = .547$

48. χ^2 observed = 7.63 χ^2 critical = 5.991 $V = .226$

Test Questions

1. Which level of measurement is appropriate for the independent and dependent variables when using a chi-square analysis?
*a. nominal
b. ordinal
c. interval
d. ratio

2. Which of the following conditions would necessitate choosing a test other than chi-square test of independence?
*a. observations are within subjects.
b. the independent variable is qualitative.
c. the dependent variable is qualitative.
d. the observations on each variable are between subjects in nature.

3. A chi-square test may be used to analyze the relationship between two variables when _____.
a. both variables are qualitative in nature
b. the two variables have been measured on the same subjects
c. the observations on each variable are between-subjects in nature
*d. all of the above

4. The chi-square test is typically used to analyze the relationship between two variables when:
a. both variables are quantitative in nature and are measured on a level that at least approximates interval characteristics
b. there is an extremely small sample size
c. the observations on each variable are *within-subjects* in nature
*d. none of the above

5. The use of frequency information is predicated on the fact that the chi-square test is designed for use with _____ variables, and it is not appropriate to compute _____ for variables of this type.
a. quantitative; marginal frequencies
b. quantitative; contingency tables
*c. qualitative; means
d. qualitative; degrees of freedom

6. The basis of analysis for the chi-square test is a(n) _____ table (also called a *frequency* or *crosstabulation table*).
a. expected frequency
b. cellular
c. summary
*d. contingency

7. Each unique combination of _____ in a contingency table is referred to as a(n) _____.
*a. variables; cell
b. cells; variable
c. rows; cell
d. cells; expected frequency

8. The entries within the cells of a contingency table represent the number of individuals in the sample who are characterized by the corresponding levels of the _____ and are referred to as _____.
a. marginal frequencies; observed frequencies
b. contingency table; unexpected frequencies
c. variables; expected frequencies
*d. variables; observed frequencies

9. The sum of the frequencies in the corresponding row or column are referred to as:
a. observed frequencies
*b. marginal frequencies
c. expected frequencies
d. total frequencies

10. If subjects in a gender and political party identification study were selected for participation without regard to gender or political party identification, the marginal frequencies for both of these variables would be:
a. fixed
b. constrained
*c. random
d. unidentified

11. When the marginal frequencies of both variables under study are random, the test is known as the chi-square test of:
a. heterogeneity
b. dependence
*c. independence
d. homogeneity

12. When the marginal frequencies are random for one variable and fixed for the other, the test is referred to as the chi-square test of:
a. heterogeneity
b. dependence
c. independence
*d. homogeneity

13. Which of the following situations refers to a chi-square test of independence?
*a. when the marginal frequencies of both variables are random
b. when one of the marginal frequencies for a variable is fixed
c. when both of the variables have marginal frequencies that are fixed
d. all of the above

14. Which of the following situations refers to a chi-square test of homogeneity?
a. when the marginal frequencies of both variables are random
*b. when one of the marginal frequencies for a variable is fixed but the other is random
c. when both the variables have marginal frequencies that are fixed
d. all of the above apply

15. As the observed and expected frequencies become more dissimilar, then we are more likely to _____.
a. accept the null
*b. reject the null
c. increase the sample size
d. reject H_1

16. In a chi-square test, the null hypothesis states that _____.
a. the two variables of interest are related in the population
*b. the two variables of interest are unrelated in the population
c. the column frequencies equal the row frequencies
d. the sum of the row and column frequencies equal the total frequency

17. The alternative hypothesis for chi-square test states that _____.
*a. the two variables of interest are related in the population
b. the two variables of interest are unrelated in the population
c. the column frequencies equal the row frequencies
d. the sum of the row and column frequencies equals the total frequency

18. The alternative hypothesis in a chi-square test is _____.
*a. nondirectional
b. directional

19. As the discrepancy between the observed and expected frequencies becomes larger, the magnitude of the chi-square statistic _____.
a. decreases
b. does not change
*c. increases
d. increases by a factor of the square of the difference

Use the following information for Questions 20-23.

In a study of the relationship between pigmentation and type of startle reactions (that is, freeze or flee) of 68 different bird species, a comparative psychologist observed the following frequency data:

	Degree of Pigmentation		
Startle Response	Light	Medium	Dark
Freeze	16	7	6
Flee	5	11	23

20. The expected frequency for the lightly pigmented birds that froze when startled may be calculated as _____.
a. 29×(16/29)   c. 21×(16/29)
b. 29×(16/68)   *d. 29×(21/68)

21. The expected frequency for the darkly pigmented birds that fled when startled may be calculated as _____.
a. (23/29)×68   c. (23/29)×68
b. (29/39)/68   *d. (29/68)×39

22. The chi-square statistic for the above data is _____.
*a. 15.47   c. 21.64
b. 68   d. none of the above

23. The strength of the relationship, as indexed by Cramer's V, is _____.
a. .56   b. .34   *c. .48   d. .23

24. The alternative hypothesis for the chi-square test is _____ in nature.
a. directional   c. mathematical
*b. nondirectional   d. computational

25. Application of the chi-square test requires computation of a(n) _____ for each cell under the assumption of no relationship between the two variables.
*a. expected frequency   c. mean
b. observed frequency   d. standard error

26. The chi-square statistic is an index that reflects the overall difference between the _____ and the _____ frequencies.
a. observed; total   c. expected; marginal
*b. observed; expected   d. expected; total

27. If two variables are unrelated in the population, the _____ value of chi-square will equal _____.
a. sample; 0
b. population; 1.0
c. sample; 1.0
*d. population; 0

28. Because of sampling error, a chi-square computed from sample data might be _____ even when the null hypothesis is true.
a. less than 0
b. uninterpretable
*c. greater than 0

29. There are different chi-square distributions depending on the _____ associated with them.
a. standard errors
b. marginal frequencies
c. number of cells
*d. degrees of freedom

30. One of the assumptions of the chi-square test is that the *expected* frequency for each cell is:
a. zero
*b. nonzero
c. independent
d. random

31. Although the issue is controversial, statisticians generally recommend that the lowest _____ one should have in order to use the chi-square statistic is somewhere around _____.
*a. expected frequency; 5
b. observed frequency; 20
c. number of cells; 5
d. degrees of freedom; 10

32. As long as the _____ assumption is met, observed frequencies can be as low as _____.
a. homogeneity of variance; 10
b. normality; 1.0
c. observed frequency; 0
*d. expected frequency; 0

33. When both of the variables under study have only two levels, the sampling distribution of the chi-square statistic corresponds _____ to a chi-square distribution than when one or both variables have more than two levels.
a. more precisely
b. exactly
c. more closely
*d. less closely

34. Recent studies have shown that Yates' correction of continuity should *not* be used, as it tends to reduce _____ with little gain over _____ control.
a. cell frequencies; standard error
b. alpha levels; statistical
*c. statistical power; Type I error
d. sample size; random error

35. Research has generally found _____ to be preferable to the chi-square test in small sample situations.
a. Yates' Correction for Continuity
*b. Fisher's Exact Test
c. Fisher's alpha test
d. none of the above

36. As the degrees of freedom increase, the shape of the sampling distribution of the chi-square statistic will become more _____.
a. positively skewed
b. negatively skewed
*c. normal in shape
d. peaked in shape

37. When the degrees of freedom of a chi-square statistic are small (for example, 2), the shape of the sampling distribution will be _____.
*a. extremely positively skewed
b. highly negatively skewed
c. very normal
d. unknown

38. The degrees of freedom for the chi-square statistic for the test of independence depends on the _____.
*a. number of levels of both variables
b. sample size
c. number of levels of the independent variable
d. number of levels of the dependent variable

39. Using Table J, what decision would you make if you observed a chi-square statistic was 36.08 and your sample size was 20?
a. p<.05, reject H_0
b. p<.02, reject H_0
c. p>.01, fail to reject H_0
*d. need more information

40. Which of the following is not an assumption of the chi-square test?
a. The observations are independently drawn from the population
b. The observations are randomly sampled from the population
*c. The observed frequency of any cell must be greater than zero
d. The expected frequency of each cell is nonzero

41. Which of the following is the recommended lowest expected frequency per cell one should have in order to use the chi-square test?
a. 0
*b. 5
c. .5
d. none of the above

42. When analyzing data from a 2×2 contingency table, a correction factor has been suggested so that _____.
*a. the sampling distribution better approximates the chi-square distribution
b. the power to reject the null increases
c. the degrees of freedom are correct
d. all of the above

43. Yates' correction for continuity involves which of the following procedures?
a. subtracting 5 from the absolute value of $|O_j-E_j|$
*b. subtracting .5 from the absolute value of $|O_j-E_j|$
c. subtracting .5 from the absolute value of $|O_j-E_j|^2$
d. subtracting 5 from the absolute value of $|O_j-E_j|^2$

44. Which of the following occurs when using Yates' correction procedure?
a. The power of the chi-square test increases.
b. The degrees of freedom are further reduced.
*c. The power of the chi-square is reduced.
d. None of the above.

45. If the data from a 3×2 contingency table resulted an observed chi-square statistic of 10.00 with a N of 111, what is the value of Cramer's statistic?
a. $\sqrt{.9}$
b. $\sqrt{.045}$
c. ,09
*d. .30

46. Which of the following indices measure the strength of the relationship between two variables in a contingency table when both variables have three levels?
a. the phi coefficient
b. Pearson correlation
*c. Cramer's statistic
d. the fourfold point correlation coefficient

47. The fourfold point correlation coefficient is used when _____.
a. one of the variables has three levels
b. both of the variables have three or more levels
c. the variables are ordinal in nature
*d. both variables have two levels each

48. If a variable has been measured on a multi-valued quantitative scale, then creating categories and using a chi-square procedure will usually _____.
a. violate the assumptions of the chi square test
*b. result in using a less powerful statistical test than alternatives
c. increase the sensitivity of the test
d. none of the above

49. When trying to decide the sample size necessary to achieve a particular level of statistical power, what information is needed?
a. size of the contingency table
b. population value of Cramer's statistic
c. the alpha level
*d. all of the above

50. The most common index of the strength of the relationship between two variables in a contingency table is the:
a. fourfold point correlation coefficient
b. Cramér's statistic
*c. a and b
d. neither a nor b

51. The test of the chi-square statistic applies to the data as a whole and provides _____ as to which cells are causing rejection of H_0.
*a. no information
b. partial information
c. complete information
d. none of the above

52. From an intuitive perspective, insight into the nature of the relationship can be gained by examining the _____ and _____ values for each cell.
a. observed; expected
*b. O-E; (O-E)²/E
c. O-E; E^2
d. overall F; χ^2

53. The power of the chi-square test is further reduced when quantitative variables are collapsed into categories because _____ by placing individuals with different scores into the same group.
*a. considerable information is likely to be lost
b. more Type I errors are likely to be made
c. sampling difficulties may arise
d. all of the above

54. The question addressed by the _____ test is whether a distribution of frequencies across categories for a variable in a population are distributed in a specified manner.
a. nonparametric
*b. goodness-of-fit
c. F
d. distribution-specific

55. For the chi-square goodness-of-fit test, statisticians recommend that the lowest _____ frequency of any cell be between 5 and 10 in a 2X2 table and 5 in larger tables.
a. unexpected
b. total
c. observed
*d. expected

Chapter 16: Nonparametric Statistical Tests

Comments to Instructors

This chapter covers a great deal of material in a short amount of space. Most of the material is straightforward, if a student has mastered previous chapters in the textbook. However, there is a large amount of information. What is most important from a "big picture" perspective is that the student be able to accurately identify the parametric and nonparametric counterparts to each other (e.g., the Wilcoxon rank sum test is the counterpart to the independent groups t test) and that he or she knows how to answer the three basic questions about relationships for any given nonparametric test.

Examples for Class

To develop applications for this chapter, I use the data and research from the chapter that presented the parametric counterpart to the nonparametric test. This allows me to illustrate what happens when you apply nonparametric methods to the same data as a parametric method. These examples often yield tied ranks. I either apply the correction formulas presented in the appendix to the chapter or I perform the analyses without the correction, noting to students that the correction factor would not change results appreciably (which is typically the case unless more than 25% of the data are involved in ties). Alternatively, the examples from Chapter 16 in the main textbook can be used, where no ties occur, although there is then some redundancy.

Answers to Selected Exercises

11. $R_P = 35$ $R_N = 2 = T$
    critical $T = 3$ reject H_0

12. $r_C = .917$

13. H = .335   Since H observed (.335) < H critical (5.991), fail to reject H_0.

14. $E_R^2 = .01$

27. a

29. b

33. b

35. d

41. $R_1 = 95$ $R_2 = 158$ E = 115 $\sigma_R = 15.17$ z = -1.3188

44. $\chi^2 = 10.4$ Since χ^2 observed (10.4) > χ^2 critical (5.991), reject H_0.
    W = .52

45. r_S = .764
    s_{rs} = .152
    t = 5.026   Since t observed (5.026) > t critical (2.101), reject H_0.

Test Questions

1. Another name for nonparametric statistical tests is a(n) ____.
*a. distribution-free   c. robust
b. nonrandom-distribution   d. unbiased

2. Distribution-free tests are used when ____.
a. samples are larger than 40
*b. parametric assumptions are markedly violated
c. data are normally distributed
d. none of the above

3. A nonparametric statistical test will typically be used when data are measured at the ___ or ___ level.
a. nominal; interval
*b. nominal; ordinal
c. ordinal; ratio
d. interval; ratio

4. Two types of nonparametric tests are ___ and ___ tests.
a. frequency; rank
b. frequency; sign
c. rank; variance
*d. rank; sign

5. You are given the following data:

Subject	1	2	3	4	5
Score	10	12	8	10	2
Rank	--	--	--	--	--

The ranks for the scores of subjects 1-5 are ___.
*a. 3.5, 5, 2, 3.5, 1
b. 1, 2, 3.5, 3.5, 5
c. 3, 5, 2, 4, 1
d. none of the above

6. Statistical tests that require assumptions about the distribution of scores in the populations from which the samples are selected are called ___ statistical tests.
a. robust
b. distributional
*c. parametric
d. nonparametric

7. ___ statistical tests are a class of statistics that, in general, make few, if any, distributional assumptions
a. nonparametric
b. distribution-free
c. parametric
*d. a and b

8. Nonparametric tests can be used to analyze ___ variables that are measured on a(n) ___ level.
*a. quantitative; ordinal
b. qualitative; interval
c. quantitative; nominal
d. all of the above

9. Rather than comparing groups in terms of _____, the nonparametric procedures compare groups in terms of _____ or other features of a distribution.
a. medians; means
*b. means; medians
c. modes; means
d. means; variances

10. If one wants to compare the rank ordering of scores as a function of different groups, then a(n) _____ should be used.
*a. nonparametric test
b. parametric test
c. t test
d. F test

11. Most of the parametric tests that we have considered have a nonparametric counterpart in the sense that the structure of the _____ is comparable across the two methods of analysis.
a. summary table
b. underlying distribution
c. critical ratio
*d. independent variable

12. There are two major types of nonparametric counterparts to parametric test: _____ tests and _____ tests.
a. robust; nonrobust
b. significance; nonsignificance
*c. rank; signed
d. signed; unsigned

13. In cases where a tie occurs, the tied scores are assigned the _____ of the ranks involved.
a. highest
*b. average
c. lowest
d. mode

14. The most common approach to dealing with tied scores is to rank the scores by assigning the average rank for ties and then to introduce a(n) _____ into the formula for the test statistic to adjust for the presence of ties.
*a. correction term
b. error term
c. nonparametric term
d. rank-order term

15. A benefit of many nonparametric statistical tests is their relative lack of sensitivity to:
a. standard errors
b. slightly skewed distributions
c. error scores
*d. outliers

16. Extreme values might prove to be problematic for parametric analyses, but they pose no particular problem for many nonparametric analyses. Because of this property, nonparametric tests are often said to be:
a. robust
b. corrected
c. outlier sensitive
*d. outlier resistant

17. The _____ involves converting a set of scores on a variable to ranks and then analyzing these rank scores using the traditional parametric formulas.
a. rank order approach
*b. rank transformation approach
c. parametric approach
d. traditional approach

18. Which of the following is not a requirement for the Wilcoxon ranked-sum test?
*a. The independent variable is within-groups or matched.
b. The independent variable has two levels.
c. The dependent variable is measured at the ordinal level.
d. The R statistic is normally distributed.

19. Which of the following is not a requirement for the Mann-Whitney U?
a. The independent variable must be between-subjects.
*b. The independent variable must be qualitative.
c. The dependent variable is measured at the ordinal level.
d. The independent variable has only two levels.

20. The Wilcoxon rank sum test and the Mann-Whitney U test are the nonparametric counterparts of the:
a. one-sample z test
b. correlated groups t test
*c. independent groups t test
d. none of the above

21. When one or both sample sizes are smaller than 10, the sampling distribution of the R statistic does not approximate a normal distribution, so application of the _____ is not appropriate.
*a. Wilcoxon rank sum test
b. Mann-Whitney U test
c. multiple R test
d. none of the above

22. When the data are analyzed using the Mann-Whitney U test, the observed U statistic is statistically significant if it is ____ the critical U.
a. equal to
b. less than
*c. equal to or less than
d. greater than

23. The Wilcoxon signed-rank test is the nonparametric counterpart of the:
a. one-sample z test
*b. correlated groups t test
c. independent groups t test
d. F test

24. The Wilcoxon signed-rank test is typically used to analyze the relationship between two variables when:
a. scores on the dependent variable are in the form of ranked differences
b. the independent variable is within-subjects in nature
c. the independent variable has two and only two levels
*d. all of the above

25. The ____ of the relationship for the Wilcoxon signed-rank test can be measured using the matched-pairs rank biserial correlation coefficient.
a. nature
*b. strength
c. existence
d. form

26. The nature of the relationship between the two variables for the Wilcoxon signed-rank test is addressed by inspection of the:
*a. rank sums
b. sum of squared ranks
c. mean ranks
d. group means

27. The ____ should be used when (1) the scores for the dependent variable are in the form of ranks, (2) the independent variable is between-subjects, and (3) the independent variable has three or more levels.
a. Mann-Whitney U test
b. Spearman correlation
c. Friedman analysis
*d. Kruskal-Wallis test

Use the following data to answer questions 28-31.

Mr. Smith, a first grade teacher, wants to determine the best technique for teaching vocabulary words. He randomly assigns his 15 students to 1 of 3 groups. Group 1 repeats each word of a 20-item list verbally and spells it 10 times. Group 2 writes each word 10 times. Group 3 makes up 10 sentences for each word. When the students take the vocabulary test, they are ranked from 1 to 15 (lowest to highest score). The rank data follow:

Student's Class Rank for Spelling Test
Verbal repetition   2, 6, 8, 10, 4
Written repetition   1, 2, 5, 7, 9
Making sentences   11, 12, 13, 14, 15

28. Which statistical test should be used to determine if the techniques are equally effective?
a. Mann-Whitney U   c. Friedman ANOVA
b. Wilcoxon rank   *d. Kruskal-Wallis

29. The value obtained for the test statistic is ___.
*a. 9.5   b. 10.6   c. 8.4   d. 2.6

30. The df for the "vocabulary test" data is ___.
a. 14   *b. 2   c. 12   d. 4

31. If a significant difference does exist between the 3 groups, a ____ procedure should be used to determine which groups are significantly different.
a. Friedman's   c. X^2
*b. Dunn's   d. Cramèr's

32. Following a significant Mann-Whitney U test, the strength of the relationship between two variables may be measured using ___.
*a. Glass rank biserial correlation coefficient
b. matched-pairs rank biserial correlation coefficient
c. epsilon-squared
d. Dunn's procedure

33. The strength of the relationship for the Wilcoxon signed-rank test can be measured using the ____.
*a. matched-pairs rank biserial correlation
b. epsilon-squared
c. Glass rank biserial correlation coefficient
d. none of the above

34. The nonparametric counterpart of a one-way repeated-measures ANOVA is ____.
*a. Friedman ANOVA by ranks
b. Kruskal-Wallis test
c. Mann-Whitney ANOVA
d. Wilcoxon ANOVA

Use the following data to answer questions 35-38.

Suppose seven members of a research team ranked the difficulty of learning to use three computer statistics programs. A rank of 1 was assigned to the easiest, whereas a 3 was given to the most difficult. The data follow:

Statistics Program

Member	Stat Friend	Showboat	Stat Zoo
1	2	3	1
2	1	2	3
3	1	3	2
4	1	3	2
5	1	2	3
6	2	3	1
7	1	3	2

35. What procedure should be used to determine if there are any differences in learning the different statistics programs?
*a. Friedman analysis of variance by ranks
b. Kruskal-Wallis test
c. repeated-measures ANOVA
d. Wilcoxon rank sum test

36. What is the value of the appropriate test statistic for the data set
*a. 7.14.   b. .11   c. 91.14   d. 21.68

37. Using the appropriate appendix, which of the following is the critical value for the test statistic ($\alpha = .05$)?
a. 1.386   b. 2.706   c. 3.841   *d. 5.991

38. What are the degrees of freedom for the test statistic?
a. 12   *b. 2   c. 6   d. 18

39. Which of the following conditions distinguishes a Friedman test from a Mann-Whitney U test?
*a. the number of levels of the independent variable
b. the measurement scale of the dependent variable
c. the measurement scale of the independent variable
d. all of the above

40. Which of the following conditions distinguishes a Kruskal-Wallis test from a Mann-Whitney test?
a. the measurement scale of the dependent variable
*b. the number of levels of the independent variable
c. the measurement level of independent variable
d. whether or not the independent variable is within-subjects

41. The Kruskal-Wallis test is the nonparametric counterpart of the:
a. one-way repeated measures analysis of variance
*b. one-way between-subjects analysis of variance
c. independent groups t test
d. correlated groups t test

42. The _____ involves using the Wilcoxon rank sum test or the Mann-Whitney U test to compare the mean ranks for all possible pairs of conditions.
a. epsilon procedure   c. Tukey HSD
b. pairwise procedure   *d. Dunn procedure

43. The Friedman analysis of variance by ranks is the nonparametric counterpart of the:
*a. one-way repeated measures analysis of variance
b. one-way between-subjects analysis of variance
c. independent groups *t* test
d. correlated groups *t* test

44. The Friedman analysis of variance by ranks is typically used to analyze the relationship between two variables when:
a. scores on the dependent variable are in the form of ranks across conditions for each subject
b. the independent variable is within-subjects in nature
c. the independent variable has three or more levels
*d. all of the above

45. The Spearman rank-order correlation is a nonparametric counterpart of the:
a. one-way repeated measures analysis of variance
*b. Pearson correlation
c. independent groups *t* test
d. coefficient of determination

46. The Spearman rank-order correlation is typically used to analyze the relationship between two variables when:
a. scores on both variables are in the form of ranks
b. the two variables have been measured on the same individuals
c. the observations on each variable are within-subjects in nature
*d. a and b

47. An alternative index of correlation of ranked scores is a statistic proposed by Kendall called:
a. sigma   *c. tau
b. delta   d. gamma

Chapter 17: Two Way Between-Subjects Analysis of Variance

Comments to Instructors

One of the most difficult concepts for students to grasp is that of an interaction effect. In addition to the material in the text, I characterize interaction effects as *moderated* relationships, and diagram them, conceptually, as follows:

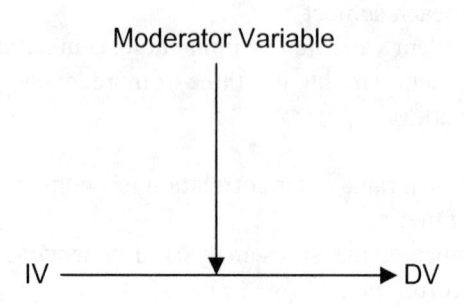

```
            Moderator Variable
                    |
                    |
                    v
       IV ─────────────────────> DV
```

The arrows indicate the hypothesized presence of a causal relationship between variables (e.g., the arrow from the independent variable, IV, and the dependent variable, DV, indicates that the IV causes the DV). In the moderator approach, one of the two factors in the factorial design is designated the independent variable and the other factor is designated the moderator variable. The moderator variable is said to influence either the strength or the nature of the relationship between the independent variable and the dependent variable (hence the arrow going to the arrow). For example, using the example in the textbook, suppose that the independent variable is religion, the dependent variable is the number of children someone wants to have, and the moderator variable is religiosity. In the above diagram, religiosity is said to moderate the impact of religion on the number of preferred children. For example, it may be that there are differences in the preferred number of children between Catholics and Protestants for religious individuals, but not for non-religious individuals. In this case, the effect of religion on the preferred number of children *depends upon* religiosity. The choice of which variable is conceptualized as the moderator variable and which as the primary independent variable does not matter statistically, but it may be important from a theoretical standpoint. It may help students to think of interaction effects in terms of moderator variables.

Another common point of confusion is with respect to the follow-up tests to determine the nature of a relationship for a statistically significant main effect. Some students try to apply the Tukey HSD test when the main effect has only two levels.

There are many formulas and calculations in this chapter and there is a risk of students losing sight of the bigger picture. Don't let them!

Examples for Class

To develop the logic of factorial analysis of variance, I use a 2x3 analysis of variance. The study focuses on educational messages provided to high school students about drunk driving and alcohol use. The first factor is how the information contained in the message is framed. When discussing the consequences of alcohol use and drunk driving, one can either emphasize the positive consequences of not engaging in the behavior or the negative consequences of engaging in the behavior. Both strategies focus on the same information, but the former uses a "positive" frame of reference and the latter a "negative" frame of reference. The research question is which will be more effective, if either. The second factor is the source of the message. The (identical) message is attributed to either a peer, a peer who is a recovered alcoholic, or a health professional. The research question is whether a peer will be more influential than an adult (even when the identical message is presented), and whether knowledge of the drinking history of the peer will impact on message effectiveness.

Students were provided a two page pamphlet to read that conformed to one of the cells of the design. One week after reading it, they were given a recall test to see how many points they could correctly recall from it. Recall scores could range from 0 to 25, with higher scores indicating better recall. Here are the data:

	Peer	Recovered Peer	Professional
Positive	7, 8, 9, 10, 11	6, 7, 8, 9, 10	5, 6, 7, 8, 9
Negative	7, 8, 9, 10, 11	14, 15, 16, 17, 18	3, 4, 5, 6, 7

This yields the following means:

	Peer	Recovered Peer	Professional	Total
Positive	9.0	8.0	7.0	8.0
Negative	9.0	16.0	5.0	10.0
Total	9.0	12.0	6.0	

The grand mean is 9.0 and the standard deviation estimate within each cell is 1.58. The summary table is:

Source	SS	df	MS	F
Frame (A)	30.00	1	30.00	12.00**
Source (B)	180.00	2	90.00	36.00**
AxB	140.00	2	70.00	28.00**
Within	60.00	24	2.50	
Total	410.00	29		

** $p < .01$

$Eta^2_A = .073$ $Eta^2_B = .439$ $Eta^2_{AxB} = .341$

For the main effect of source, the value of CD for the Tukey HSD test is 1.765. For the interaction comparisons, we obtain the following:

Subtable 1

	Peer	Recov Peer
Pos	9.0	8.0
Neg	9.0	16.0

Subtable 2

	Peer	Prof
Pos	9.0	7.0
Neg	9.0	5.0

Subtable 3

	Recov Peer	Prof
Pos	8.0	7.0
Neg	16.0	5.0

$SS_{AxB(1)} = 80.00$ $SS_{AxB(2)} = 5.00$ $SS_{AxB(3)} = 125.00$

Contrast	F ratio	p value	Critical alpha
$AXB_{(3)}$	50.00	<.000001	.05/3 = .0167
$AXB_{(1)}$	20.00	.000159	.05/2 = .025
$AXB_{(2)}$	2.00	.170142	.05/1 = .05

As a second example, I use a 2x2 design in which personnel managers are asked to review an application file for a job applicant and then to rate the likelihood that they would hire the applicant, using a 0 to 100 scale (with higher numbers indicating a greater likelihood). The case descriptions of the applicant are identical for all managers except that for half the managers the applicant is identified as being a male and for the other half, the applicant is identified as being female. In addition, a photograph of the applicant accompanying the materials is either that of an attractive individual or an unattractive individual. This yields a 2x2 design. Here are the data:

	Attractive	Unattractive
Male	60, 65, 70, 75, 80	50, 55, 60, 65, 70
Female	50, 55, 60, 65, 70	20, 25, 30, 35, 40

This yields the following means:

	Attractive	Unattractive	Total
Male	70.00	60.00	65.00
Female	60.00	30.00	45.00
Total	65.00	45.00	

The grand mean is 55.00. The summary table is:

Source	SS	df	MS	F
Gender (A)	2,000.00	1	2,000.00	32.00**
Attractiveness (B)	2,000.00	1	2,000.00	32.00**
AxB	500.00	1	500.00	8.00*
Within	1,000.00	16	62.50	
Total	5,500.00	19		

* p <.05; ** p < .01

$Eta^2_A = .364$ $Eta^2_B = .364$ $Eta^2_{AxB} = .091$

The main effects indicate that males are more likely to be hired than females and that attractive applicants are more likely to be hired than unattractive applicants. The interaction indicates that attractiveness has a larger effect for females than for males.

Answers to Selected Exercises

14.
Source	SS	df	MS	F
A	14.00	2	7.00	3.50
B	12.00	2	6.00	3.00
A X B	40.00	4	10.00	5.00
Within	54.00	27	2.00	
Total	120.00	35		

27. Observed $F(1, 24) = 10.00$ critical $F(1, 24) = 4.26$
    $\overline{X}$ for $A_1 = 12.00$ $\overline{X}$ for $A_2 = 8.00$

28. Since F observed (.83) is less than 1.00, it cannot be statistically significant.

29. Observed $F(2, 24) = 15.83$ critical $F(2, 24) = 3.40$

Contrast	F ratio	p value	Critical alpha
$AXB_{(2)}$	15.00	<.001	.05/3 = .0167
$AXB_{(1)}$	3.75	.063	.05/2 = .025
$AXB_{(3)}$	3.75	.063	.05/1 = .05

30.
Source	SS	df	MS	F
A	3.025	1	3.025	3.225
B	4.675	3	1.558	1.661
AxB	17.075	3	5.692	6.068
Within	30.00	32	.938	
Total	54.775	39		

critical $F(1, 32) = 4.15$ — no significant main effect of gender

critical $F(3, 32) = 2.90$ — no significant main effect of academic major

critical $F(3, 32) = 2.90$ — significant interaction between gender and academic major

31. $eta^2 A = .055$ $eta^2 B = .085$ $eta^2 AxB = .312$

33. Because there was no statistically significant main effect of academic major, one can conclude that there is no relationship between academic major and number of job offers. Therefore, it is not appropriate to carry out the Tukey HSD test.

34.
Contrast	F ratio	p value	Critical alpha
$AXB_{(5)}$	13.62	.001	$.05/6 = .0083$
$AXB_{(3)}$	10.43	.003	$.05/5 = .01$
$AXB_{(4)}$	6.44	.016	$.05/4 = .0125$
$AXB_{(2)}$	4.31	.046	$.05/3 = .0167$
$AXB_{(6)}$	1.33	.257	$.05/2 = .025$
$AXB_{(1)}$	.213	.647	$.05/1 = .05$

50.
Source	SS	df	MS	F
A (Race)	80.00	1	80.00	71.11
B (Intelligence)	45.00	1	45.00	40.00
A x B	20.00	1	20.00	17.78
Within	18.00	16	1.13	
Total	163.00	19		

critical $F(1, 16) = 4.49$ significant main effect of race

$\overline{X}$ for blacks = 29.50
$\overline{X}$ for whites = 33.50

critical $F(1, 16) = 4.49$ significant main effect of intelligence

$\overline{X}$ for gifted = 33.00
$\overline{X}$ for nongifted = 30.00

critical $F(1, 16) = 4.49$ significant interaction between race and intelligence

$\overline{X}$ for black/gifted = 30.00
$\overline{X}$ for black/nongifted = 29.00
$\overline{X}$ for white/gifted = 36.00
$\overline{X}$ for white/nongifted = 31.00

eta^2 A (Race) = .49 eta^2 B (Intelligence) = .28
eta^2 AxB = .12

The effect of race on interaction is more pronounced for gifted children (30.00 - 36.00 = -6.00) than for nongifted children (29.00 - 31.00 = -2.00). Or, the effect of intelligence on interaction is more pronounced among whites (36.00 - 31.00 = 5.00) than blacks (30.00 - 29.00 = 1.00).

51.
Source	SS	df	MS	F
A (Video)	94.89	2	47.44	82.91
B (Gender)	0.03	1	0.03	0.05
A x B	0.89	2	0.44	0.78
Within	17.17	30	0.57	
Total	112.97	35		

critical $F(2, 30) = 3.32$ significant main effect of video

$\overline{X}$ for no video = 6.25
$\overline{X}$ for mildly aggressive video = 9.08
$\overline{X}$ for highly aggressive video = 10.08

critical $F(1, 30) = 4.17$ no significant main effect of gender

$\overline{X}$ for males = 8.44
$\overline{X}$ for females = 8.50

critical $F(2, 16) = 3.32$ no significant interaction between video and gender

$\overline{X}$ for no video/males = 6.00
$\overline{X}$ for no video/females = 6.50
$\overline{X}$ for mildly aggressive video/males = 9.17
$\overline{X}$ for mildly aggressive video/females = 9.00
$\overline{X}$ for highly aggressive video/males = 10.17
$\overline{X}$ for mildly aggressive video/females = 10.00

eta^2 A (Video) = .84
eta^2 B (Gender) = .0003
eta^2 AxB = .008

For the effect of video, CD for Tukey test = .63

52.
Source	SS	df	MS	F
A (Details)	12.39	2	6.19	7.12
B (Mode)	2.89	2	1.44	1.66
A x B	2.78	4	0.69	0.79
Within	23.50	27	0.87	
Total	41.56	35		

critical $F(2, 27) = 3.35$ significant main effect of details

$\overline{X}$ for none = 5.67
$\overline{X}$ for small = 4.75
$\overline{X}$ for large = 4.25

critical $F(2, 27) = 3.35$ no significant main effect of mode

$\overline{X}$ for e mail = 5.17
$\overline{X}$ for phone = 4.50
$\overline{X}$ for note = 5.00

critical $F(4, 27) = 2.73$ no significant interaction between details and mode

$\overline{X}$ for no details, e mail = 6.25
$\overline{X}$ for no details, phone = 4.75
$\overline{X}$ for no details, note = 6.00
$\overline{X}$ for small details, e mail = 5.00
$\overline{X}$ for small details, phone = 4.50
$\overline{X}$ for small details, note = 4.75
$\overline{X}$ for large details, e mail = 4.25
$\overline{X}$ for large details, phone = 4.25
$\overline{X}$ for large details, note = 4.25

eta^2 A (deatils) = 0.30
eta^2 B (mode) = 0.07
eta^2 AxB = 0.07

For the effect of details, CD for Tukey test = .945

Test Questions

1. One statistical technique for analyzing the relationship between a dependent variable and two or more independent variables is ____.
a. rank-order correlation
*b. two-way between-subjects analysis of variance
c. repeated measures analysis of variance
d. Kruskal-Wallis analysis of variance

2. The joint effect of two independent variables on a dependent variable is indicated by the ____ effect when a two-way factorial analysis is used.
a. main   c. significant
b. simple   *d. interaction

For questions 3 and 4: Dr. Fleet is interested in studying the effect of gender, years of undergraduate college (0-4 years), and marital status (single, married, divorced, or widowed) on the annual income of residents of the northeastern United States.

3. Which of the following describes a design that she might use?
a. 2 x 2 factorial design
*b. 2 x 5 x 4 factorial design
c. 2 x 2 repeated-measures design
d. 2 x 2 x 2 factorial design

4. She would have ____ groups of subjects to study.
a. 4   c. 2
*b. 40   d. 6

5. Which of the following is not a requirement for use of a two-way between-subjects factorial ANOVA?
a. The dependent variable is quantitative in nature.
b. The independent variables are each between-subjects in nature.
*c. The dependent variable must be measured on a nominal level
d. The independent variables are combined to form a factorial design.

6. The joint effects of two independent variables on a dependent variable can be studied using:
*a. factorial designs   c. single-subject designs
b. one-way analysis of variance   d. none of the above

7. Two-way factorial designs allow us to study:
a. main effects   *c. a and b
b. interaction effects

8. An interaction effect refers to the case where the nature or strength of the relationship between one of the independent variables and the dependent variable differs as a function of the:
a. sample size   c. dependent variable
b. number of variables   *d. other independent variable

9. When dealing with population means, if the lines in a graph are _____, this suggests the presence of an interaction.
*a. not parallel   c. curvilinear
b. parallel   d. none of the above

10. When dealing with sample data, the existence of a given population main effect or interaction can be affirmed only by a:
a. visual inspection of sample means
b. visual inspection of slopes
*c. significant statistical test

For questions 11-18, you may wish to delete the summary table and have the student calculate it.

Suppose that you are conducting a study to determine the effect of alcohol and gender on movie preference. After giving 30 males and females either 0, .5, or 1 ounce of alcohol in a punch you show them a violent film and ask them to rate how much they liked it on an interval scale of 1 to 10. The following data result:

	Females			Males	
0 oz	.5 oz	1.0 oz	0 oz	.5 oz	1.0 oz
2	9	8	3	6	9
3	3	9	4	5	8
5	5	10	5	8	10
3	3	9	1	6	10
9	2	10	4	6	10

Here is the relevant summary table:

Source	SS	df	MS	F
Alcohol (A)	157.07	2	78.53	22.87
Gender (G)	.83	1	.83	.24
AxG	9.87	2	4.93	1.44
Within	82.4	24	3.43	

Critical values for ANOVA tests at $\alpha = .05$:

$F(1, 24) = 4.26$; $F(2, 24) = 3.4$; q for 2,24 df = 4.37

Mean ratings for the various groups

	Alcohol			
	0	.5	1.0	$\overline{X}$
Gender				
Males	3.4	6.2	9.4	6.3
Females	4.4	4.4	9.2	6.0
$\overline{X}$	3.9	5.3	9.0	

11. Which of the following hypotheses indicates that alcohol has no effect on a person's opinion of a movie?
*a. $\mu_0 = \mu_{.5} = \mu_{1.0}$
b. All μ's are not equal.
c. $\mu_0 = \mu_{.5} > \mu_{1.0}$
d. None of the above.

12. ____ is the value for the sum of squares due to gender
a. 22.874   *b. .833   c. 9.867   d. 82.4

13. ____ is the value for the degrees of freedom for gender
a. 29   b. 2   c. 24   *d. 1

14. ____ is the value of the F test for gender
*a. .243   b. .833   c. 1.437   d. 9.867

15. The degrees of freedom for the main effect of alcohol are ____ and ____.
a. 1; 29   b. 1; 24   c. 2; 29   *d. 2; 24

16. Using $\alpha = .05$, which of the following statements concerning Tukey's HSD test is correct?
*a. The HSD test should be performed in order to determine the nature of the main effect of alcohol.
b. The HSD test should be performed to determine the nature of the effect of gender
c. The HSD test should be done to determine the nature of the interaction effect
d. There is no need to conduct the HSD test.

17. Using α = .05, which of the following conclusions is accurate?
a. There were no statistically significant effects for any of the factors.
b. Males reported statistically significantly lower ratings than females, regardless of the amount of alcohol consumed.
*c. Those who consumed 1.0 oz gave statistically significantly higher mean ratings than those who consumed 0 or .5 oz.
d. Males who consumed .5 oz of alcohol reported a statistically significantly higher rating than males who drank no alcohol.

18. An eta^2 of .63 for the alcohol main effect would indicate that ____ of the variability in movie preference can be attributed to the main effect for amount of alcohol consumed.
a. 40%   *b. 63%   c. 37%   d. 79%

For questions 19-24: An organizational psychologist studying human factors conducts an experiment to determine the effect of the shape of the instrument panel and temperature of the cockpit on pilot reaction time. She tests 500 pilots and obtains the following ANOVA table.

Source	SS	df	MS	F
Temperature (T)	121.90	--	40.63	--
Shape (S)	60.70	3	--	--
T x S	--	9	15.90	--
Within	--	484	.18	
Total	--	--		

19. ____ is the SS$_{TxS}$
a. 20.30   b. 182.60   *c. 143.10   d. 60.83

20. ____ is the df$_{TEMPERATURE}$.
a. 12   b. 6   c. 1   *d. 3

21. ____ is the df$_{TOTAL}$.
a. 497   b. 493   *c. 499   d. 471

22. ____ is the MS$_{SHAPE}$.
*a. 20.2   b. 13.52   c. 162.5   d. 56.71

23. ____ is the $F_{TEMPERATURE}$.
*a. 225.7   b. 2.55   c. 20.28   d. 10.07

24. Which of the following statements are correct for $\alpha = .05$?
a. neither the shape of the instrument panel nor the temperature of the cockpit has a statistically significant effect on the mean reaction time of pilots
*b. in the population, the effect of the shape of the panel varies as a function of the temperature (barring a Type I error)
c. neither a nor b is correct.
d. both a and b are correct.

25. Which of the following statements is correct concerning the line graph of a statistically significant interaction effect when a 2 × 2 between-subjects factorial design is used?
a. The slope of each line is very steep.
*b. The lines are not parallel.
c. The y values are constant on one line and vary on the other line.
d. The slope of one of the lines is 0 (flat).

26. The total variability of a 2 × 2 factorial ANOVA can be described as ____.
a. $SS_{TOTAL} = SS_A + SS_{WITHIN}$
*b. $SS_{TOTAL} = SS_A + SS_B + SS_{A \times B} + SS_{WITHIN}$
c. $SS_{TOTAL} = SS_A + SS_B + SS_{A \times B} + SS_{A \times B \times WITHIN}$
*d. both a and b

27. The F test statistic for a main effect of factor A of a 2 × 2 factorial ANOVA is determined by which of the following formulas?
a. MS_A/df_A
b. MS_A/SS_A
*c. $MS_A/MS_{WITHIN\ GROUP}$
d. $SS_A/df_{WITHIN\ GROUP}$

28. The sum of squares between in a two-way between-subjects analysis of variance can be partitioned into:
a. $SS_A + SS_B$
*b. $SS_A + SS_B + SS_{A \times B}$
c. $SS_A + SS_{ERROR}$
d. none of the above

29. The F ratio formed by SS_A/SS_{WITHIN} is used to test the null hypothesis with respect to:
a. factor A
b. factor B
c. factors A and B
*d. none of the above

30. Which of the following formulas is incorrect?
a. $df_{WITHIN} = (a)(b)(n - 1)$
b. $df_B = b - 1$
c. $df_A = a - 1$
*d. $df_{AxB} = (a - b)$

31. The F tests for two-way between-subjects analysis of variance assume that the scores in each population:
*a. are normally distributed
b. have heterogeneous variances
c. are positively skewed
d. none of the above

32. As with one-way analysis of variance, under certain conditions the F tests are robust to violations of the _____ assumption.
a. normality
b. homogeneity of variance
*c. a and b
d. neither a nor b

33. The F test is particularly robust to violations of the normality and homogeneity of variance assumptions when sample sizes are _____ and relatively _____.
a. unequal; large
*b. equal; large
c. equal; small
d. unequal; small

34. As the number of groups in the factorial design increases, _____ becomes increasingly problematic.
a. homogeneity of population variances
*b. heterogeneity of population variances
c. non-normality
d. error variance

35. In the case of highly different sample sizes across groups, the robustness of the F test to non-normality and variance heterogeneity often _____, sometimes considerably so.
*a. diminishes
b. increases
c. fluctuates
d. none of the above

36. After a 2 × 2 factorial ANOVA has been used to determine that a statistically significant relationship exists between the dependent variable and an independent variable, a(n) ____ can be calculated to indicate the strength of the relationship.
a. t^2
*b. eta^2
b. Tukey's HSD
d. critical difference

37. A between-groups factorial ANOVA differs from a between-groups one-way ANOVA in which of the following ways?
a. two or more dependent variables are used.
b. a factorial ANOVA may produce a negative F score.
*c. two or more independent variables are used.
d. both a and b.

38. If a factorial ANOVA is computed and a statistically significant main effect is determined for a factor that has two levels, the nature of the relationship should be determined by ____.
*a. inspecting the sample means
b. calculating eta^2
c. calculating a t score
d. applying the Tukey HSD test

39. If a factorial ANOVA is conducted and a statistically significant main effect is determined for a factor that has three or more levels, the nature of the relationship should be determined by ____.
a. inspecting the sample means
b. calculating eta^2
c. calculating a between-groups ANOVA for the significant factor
*d. d. applying the Tukey HSD test

40. In a follow-up test, two population means are considered to be different if the difference between their sample means is ____ the critical difference determined by Tukey's procedure.
a. less than
c. greater than or equal to
*b. greater than
d. equal to

41. The nature of an interaction can be determined by ____.
a. eta^2
c. simple main effects
b. interaction comparisons
*d. both b and c

42. If the cells of a 2 × 2 factorial-design have unequal numbers of subjects in them, then it is common to analyze the data using
*a. simple main effects
b. least-squares analysis
c. split-plot analysis
d. nonparametric analysis

43. The strengths of the relationships for the three sources of between-group variability are assessed with:
a. eta
b. r^2
c. F^2
*d. eta-squared

44. When a statistically significant _____ effect has only two levels, the nature of the relationship is determined in the same fashion as for the independent groups t test.
a. interaction
b. simple
*c. main
d. a and b

45. If a statistically significant main effect has three or more levels, then the nature of the relationship is determined using a(n):
*a. Tukey HSD procedure
b. informal examination of sample means
c. F ratio
d. t ratio

46. In general, statisticians recommend the use of _____ over _____ in determining the nature of a statistically significant interaction effect.
a. simple main effects analysis; interaction comparisons
*b. interaction comparisons; simple main effects analysis
c. eta-squared; interaction comparisons
d. eta-squared; simple main effects analysis

47. Interaction comparisons focus on _____ within a factorial design.
a. simple main effects
b. a priori effects
c. main effects
*d. 2 X 2 subtables

48. A problem with the strategy of examining all possible 2 X 2 subtables following a significant interaction is that it does not adequately control the _____ at _____.
*a. experimentwise error rate; α c. Type II error rate; α
b. experimentwise error rate; β d. Type II error rate; β

49. The problem of an inflated Type I error rate can be controlled for interaction comparisons by using a:
a. Tukey HSD   c. corrected F ratio
*b. modified Bonferroni procedure   d. none of the above

50. Not only do factorial designs allow us to assess the interaction between the two independent variables, but they also "remove" the individual and joint effects of these variables from the:
a. between-group variability   *c. within-group variability
b. F ratio   d. sum of squares total

51. When the sample sizes are the same in all cells, the two independent variables are _____ to each other
*a. unrelated   c. positively related
b. negatively related

For questions 52-55:

Dr. Smith wants to determine if the amount of time that an animal is allowed to explore a maze will affect the animal's ability to go directly to the food dish. He also wonders if some strains of rats are better than others at the task. He uses two strains of rats and allows half of the rats to explore for 3 minutes and the other half to explore for 15 minutes. He records the amount of time(min) required for the animal to get to the food. The data are:

	Strain A		Strain B
3 min	*15 min*	*3 min*	*15 min*
45	30	22	15
40	25	25	22
42	28	27	20
49	30	30	22
48	29	24	1

ANOVA Summary Table

Source	SS	df	MS	F
Strain (S)	980.00	1	980.00	107.11
Exploration Time (E)	627.20	1	627.20	68.55
S × E	135.20	1	135.20	14.78
Within	146.40	16	9.15	

52. Which hypothesis indicates that strain has an effect on the rat's performance?
*a. $\mu_A \neq \mu_B$ c. $\mu_{A3} = \mu_{B3} = \mu_{A15} = \mu_{B15}$
b. $\mu_A = \mu_B$ d. All μ's are equal.

53. The F ratio for the main effect of exploration time is ___.
a. 14.78   b. 9.15   *c. 68.55   d. 135.20

54. The MS for the main effect of exploration time effect is ___.
a. 980.0   *b. 627.20   c. 135.20   d. 14.78

55. Which is the correct inference concerning the relationship between strain, exploration time, and time to find the food (assume that $\alpha = .05$)?
a. there are no statistically significant main effects.
*b. the effect of exploration time differs as a function of strain
c. both a and b are true.
d. neither a nor b is true.

Chapter 18: Overview and Extension

Comments to Instructors

This chapter reinforces previous decision rules for choosing a method of data analysis. I encourage my students to go to the library to get some social science journals that report empirical data (e.g., the *Journal of Experimental Psychology*, the *Journal of Experimental Social Psychology*, the *Journal of Applied Psychology*, the *Journal of Applied Social Psychology*, the *Journal of Abnormal Psychology*). I tell them to read some of the research reports and identify the method of analysis that the researchers used. I ask them to specify the criteria that probably influenced the authors' choice of analytic method, as described in this chapter. I also encourage the students to try designing some experiments of their own. After specifying the rationale, hypotheses and design, specify, what methods of data analysis would they use and why?

Examples for Class

There are no examples involving data analysis in this chapter.

Answers to Selected Exercises

There are no questions involving calculations in this chapter

Test Questions

1. Which of the following is *not* an important question when analyzing bivariate relationship?
a. Is there a relationship between the variables?
b. What is the nature of the relationship?
c. How strong is the relationship?
*d. a, b, and c are important.

2. Which of the following is a first step in determining the appropriate bivariate test?
a. Determine the number of subjects needed for a given level of power.
*b. Identify the independent and dependent variables as qualitative or quantitative.
c. Determine the appropriate alpha level.
d. Select the appropriate post hoc test.

3. A parametric procedure would not typically be used when a quantitative dependent variable has only two levels because the _____.
*a. dependent variable can not be normally distributed
b. two levels might be correlated
c. data could not be compared
d. homogeneity of variance could not be determined

4. When both of the variables under study are qualitative and between-subjects in nature, the appropriate method of data analysis is the:
*a. chi square test   c. multiple regression
b. Pearson correlation   d. none of the above

5. If both variables are qualitative, but one or both are within-subjects in nature, _____ of the statistical tests we have considered can be used.
a. all 12   c. only one
b. several   *d. none

6. The major factor to be weighed when deciding whether to use a parametric or a nonparametric test is the decision about what aspect of the _____ you want to compare groups on.
a. independent variable c. sample
*b. distribution

7. If means are the focus, then a _____ test is usually the analysis of choice.
a. chi square   *c. parametric
b. log-linear   d. nonparametric

8. If ranks are the chosen focus of study, then _____ methods should be used.
a. experimental   c. parametric
b. multiple   *d. nonparametric

9. In situations where the dependent measure has only two or three values, most researchers will *not* use a _____ test.
a. chi square   *c. parametric
b. log-linear   d. nonparametric

10. If a dependent variable turns out to be highly skewed, then it might be decided to focus on a _____ rather than a _____ to analyze the relationship between two variables.
a. mean; median   c. mean; mode
*b. median; mean   d. mode; Pearson correlation

11. If the dependent variable is measured on an ordinal level that seriously departs from _____, then a nonparametric test might be pursued instead of a parametric test.
*a. interval characteristics   c. nominal characteristics
b. normality   d. none of the above

12. A nonparametric test should be pursued if there is a reason to believe that the _____ of the corresponding parametric test have been violated to the extent that the parametric test is not robust.
a. kurtotic assumptions   c. population parameters
b. theoretical assumptions *d. distributional assumptions

13. If the dependent variable is measured on an ordinal level that seriously departs from interval characteristics, then a _____ test is typically used.
a. parametric
*b. nonparametric

14. Given two between-subjects variables that are multi-valued and measured on a level that at least approximates interval characteristics, the most common method of analysis is:
a. Spearman rank-order correlation
*b. Pearson correlation
c. point-biserial correlation
d. nonparametric correlation

15. Statistical techniques for analyzing the relationship between three or more variables are referred to as:
a. nonparametric statistics   c. multiple correlations
b. trivariate statistics   *d. multivariate statistics

16. The joint influence of two within-subjects qualitative independent variables can be studied using:
a. correlated groups t test
*b. two-way repeated measures analysis of variance
c. Hotelling T^2 test
d. factor analysis

17. The appropriate means of analysis for research designs involving one between-subjects qualitative independent variable and one within-subjects qualitative independent variable would be a:
a. log-linear analysis
*b. two-way between-within analysis of variance
c. Hotelling T^2 test
d. multiple regression

18. A _____ is often used to test whether the groups have different population means on the dependent variables considered jointly.
*a. multivariate analysis of variance
b. multiple regression
c. Hotelling T^2 test
d. factor analysis

19. When applied to a single independent variable having only two levels, multivariate analysis of variance is referred to as:
a. log-linear analysis   *c. Hotelling T^2 test
b. factor analysis   d. multiple regression

20. Statistical analyses that are designed to analyze the relationship between three or more variables simultaneously are called _____ tests.
a. interaction comparison   *c. multivariate
b. simple main effects   d. correlational

21. _____ is the statistic used to indicate the strength of relationship between a criterion variable and several predictors in the context of a linear model
a. Eta^2 *b. R^2 c. r^2

22. Multiple regression analysis involves the prediction of a _____ variable from two or more _____ variables.
a. nominal; ordinal
b. within-subjects; between-subjects
c. predictor; criterion
*d. criterion; predictor

23. In multiple regression analysis, each predictor has a "slope" (β) that is called a:
a. factor
b. squared multiple correlation coefficient
*c. regression coefficient
d. multiple r

24. An index of the strength of the relationship between the criterion variable and the set of predictor variables is provided by the ____, symbolized by ____.
a. squared t; t^2
*b. squared multiple correlation coefficient; R^2
c. regression coefficient; α
d. multiple r; r^2

25. The goal of ____ is to determine if the correlations among a set of variables can be accounted for by one or more underlying dimensions, or ____.
*a. factor analysis; factors   c. log-linear analysis; log odds
b. regression analysis; regressions   d. none of the above

26. To determine if the correlations among a set of variables can be accounted for by a one or more underlying factors, a ____ should be used.
a. log-linear analysis   c. multiple regression
*b. factor analysis   d. Spearman correlation

27. ____ will usually be applied to research questions requiring that three or more qualitative variables be simultaneously examined.
a. factor analysis
b. multivariate analysis of variance
*c. log-linear analysis
d. multiple regression

28. Alternatives to the "null hypothesis testing approach" include:
a. estimating effect sizes   *c. a and b
b. Bayesian statistics   d. none of the above

29. Some psychologists have argued that the question "is there a relationship between two variables" is meaningless, in part because:
a. psychological research is difficult to carry out
b. the alternative hypothesis is almost always false
*c. the null hypothesis is almost always false
d. empirical relationships are, in fact, very rare

For the remaining questions, assume that the distributional assumptions of the parametric procedures have been satisfied.

30. Mr. Smith believes that men are better at using maps than are women. He asks 50 females and 50 males to use a map to locate an unfamiliar location that is 60 miles away. After the participants have been gone for 1.5 hours, he will determine if they have reached the location or not. He will use the data to determine if there is a relationship between gender and map-reading ability. What is the proper statistical analysis?
a. independent-groups t
b. correlated-groups t
*c. chi-square test of homogeneity
d. Pearson correlation

31. Professor Smith has taught political science for many years. He believes that a relationship exists between a person's class standing (freshman, sophomore, junior, or senior) and their willingness to agree, at least in principle, with socialist causes. He polled 50 students from each class to determine if they would vote yes or no for a system of socialized medicine. What is the appropriate test to determine if class standing and sympathy to socialist causes are related?
*a. chi-square test of homogeneity
b. independent-groups t test
c. one way between-subjects analysis of variance
d. correlated-groups t

32. Refer to Question 31. To determine the strength of the relationship between class standing and acceptance of socialist causes, one should use _____.
*a. Cramer's statistic   c. Kruskal-Wallis H
b. eta^2 d. r^2

33. The California Highway patrol is interested in determining if age and driving speed are related. Specifically, they are interested in determining if 16-year-olds drive faster than 20-year-olds. They select 10 people from each age group and install a monitoring device that will record their driving speed at a randomly determined time on

211

a local interstate. The monitors are coded only for age; it is impossible for the patrols to identity the driver. What is the appropriate test?
a. correlated-groups t test
*b. independent-groups t test
c. chi square test of independence
d. none of the above

34. Refer to Question 33. To determine the strength of the relationship that exists between age and driving speed, one should use _____.
*a. eta^2
b. μ^2
c. r^2
d. Cramer's V

35. A company that produces table salt is interested in showing that moderate amounts of salt do not adversely affect blood pressure. Thirty subjects are randomly selected and divided into two groups. One group has a diet that contains no salt. The second group has a small predetermined amount of salt in all food. Which test should be used to determine if salt adversely affects blood pressure?
a. correlated-groups t test
*b. independent-groups t test
c. chi square test of independence
d. none of the above

36. Professor Harris wants to show that students can improve their political science grades by reading the newspaper daily. He randomly selects 30 students from the class role. He instructs 15 of them to refrain from reading any newspapers before the first exam. He instructs the others to come by his office and read the newspaper for one hour each day until the first exam. The dependent variable is the score on the first exam. Which test should he use to determine if reading the newspaper can improve one's score?
a. correlated-groups t test
*b. independent-groups t test
c. chi square test of independence
d. none of the above

37. Mr. Young is concerned that his third graders are not profiting from their physical education program. In the fall, 150 third graders are given a standard fitness exam. In the spring they are given the same exam. What test should be used to determine if their physical fitness has improved?
*a. correlated-groups t test
b. independent-groups t test
c. chi square test of independence
d. one way ANOVA

38. An oat company was asked to support its claim that its cereal product reduces cholesterol. They selected 50 people with blood cholesterol levels (BCL) that are considered to be dangerous. After their BCLs were determined, the subjects were given a month's supply of the cereal and instructed to eat one bowl per day. At the end of the month their BCLs were determined again. Which is the appropriate test to determine if oat bran decreases BCL?
*a. correlated-groups t test   c. chi square test of independence
b. independent-groups t test   d. one way ANOVA

39. Coach Jones is interested in determining if consuming a large amount of carbohydrates before a race will increase the speed of his track team. He randomly divides the team into two groups. One group eats a high-carbohydrate snack. The other group eats a low-carbohydrate snack. He then has the team run one mile. He records the order in which the 12 members finish. Which test should he use to compare the two groups?
*a. Wilcoxon signed-rank test   c. chi-square test of independence
b. Kruskal-Wallis test   d. independent-groups t

40. Professor Axelrod believes that grades on the class term paper are better when students submit them on the last day of class rather than earlier. One semester she decides to let students submit them at any time during the semester. There are 15 students in the class and for purposes of grading the papers, she ranks them from 1 to 15, best to worst. What is the appropriate test to determine if there is a relationship between the student's ranking and the day of the semester (that is, Day 1,2, 3...) that the paper is submitted?
a. correlated-groups t   c. Pearson correlation
*b. Spearman correlation   d. One way ANOVA

41. A drug company conducts a study to determine the effect of a new drug on reaction time. One hundred people are randomly selected from a local telephone directory to participate. Each person is given a different dose of the drug: (a) 0 cc, (b) .5 cc, and (c) 1.0 cc on three different days. The dependent variable is the number of milliseconds that a person takes to respond to the onset of light. What is the statistical test to determine if the drug has an effect?
a. multivariate ANOVA
b. one-way between-subjects ANOVA
*c. one-way repeated-measures ANOVA
d. three-way between-subjects ANOVA

42. Refer to Question 41. How can one determine the strength of the relationship existing between the new drug and reaction time?
a. determine Tukey's HSD   *c. determine eta^2
b. determine r^2 d. determine H^2

43. Dr. Allen is interested in determining the effect of lesions to the hippocampus on the ability of rats to go directly to food in a complicated maze. The dependent variable is the number of milliseconds that it takes an animal to find the food. One group of animals (n=50) has a damaged hippocampus; the other group (n=50) does not. What statistical test should be used to determine if the lesion has an effect at any time during the 20-day period?
a. multiple regression
b. two-way repeated-measures ANOVA
*c. one way between subjects ANOVA
d. factor analysis

44. Dr. Bennet is interested in the effects of sleep deprivation on test performance. He asks for volunteers from his introductory psychology class who will spend five nights preceding the first exam in the college sleep laboratory. He divides the 60 students who volunteer into 4 groups of 15. The sleep schedules are as follows: (1) to bed at 5:00 am up at 7:00 am; (2) to bed at 3:00 am up at 7:00 am; (3) to bed at 1:00 am up at 7:00 am; or (4) to bed at 11:00 pm up at 7:00 am. The dependent variable is the exam score. How should the relationship between the two variables be analyzed?
a. independent groups t test
b. correlated groups t test
c. one-way repeated-measures ANOVA
*d. one-way between-subjects ANOVA

45. John Morris, the director of an educational media center wants to determine the effects of audio-visual aids on a students ability to learn French. He arranges the following classroom situations: (1) lecture only; (2) lecture and audio tapes; and (3) lecture, video and audio tapes. There are 15 students in each situation. At the end of the semester the students are given a French competency exam. Which test should be used to determine the relationship between teaching method and acquisition of French?
a. independent groups t test
*b. one-way between-subjects ANOVA
c. one-way mixed ANOVA
d. one-way repeated-measures ANOVA

46. Mrs. Rogers believes that as people age they are less willing to spend money on clothes. She asks 20 individuals who range in age from 15 to 62 years to record the amount of money that they will spend for clothes during a 6 month period. What test should be used to test her hypothesis?
a. multiple regression   *c. Pearson correlation
b. Spearman correlation   d. one way ANOVA

47. Referring to Question 46, to determine the strength of the relationship between age and money spent for clothes, Mrs. Rogers should calculate ____.
a. t^2 *b. r^2 c. eta

48. Mr. Jones thinks that a person's religious preference might have an effect on his or her ability to recall events from the Bible. He finds 10 Catholics, 10 Baptists, and 10 Jews who will agree to be in his study. Rather than using the number of events remembered, Mr. Jones ranked all subjects with regard to their memory of Biblical events. Which test should he use to determine if recall ability does differ between the groups?
a. one-way between-groups ANOVA
*b. Kruskal-Wallis test
c. two-way mixed-design ANOVA
d. Friedman ANOVA by ranks

49. Professor Smith has just designed an ordinal-level humor scale that ranges from 1 to 10. He wants to determine if it will differentiate between the humorous moods of people who have seen different types of movies. Each of 30 subjects sees one type of movie-farce, mystery, or tragedy. To analyze the data, he should use _____.
a. multivariate ANOVA   *c. Kruskal-Wallis test
b. Friedman ANOVA by ranks   d. between-subjects ANOVA

50. A personnel officer is interested in finding some method by which she can predict which job applicants will be best suited for producing circuit boards. She conducts a study in which she administers 3 tests to each applicant. The tests are for manual dexterity, engineering aptitude, and critical thinking ability. After the applicants are hired, she has the number of errors that they make recorded for a 6-month period. What statistical test should she use to determine if scores on the three tests would be useful in identifying those who would be best at producing circuit boards?
a. factor analysis   c. Pearson correlation
b. Spearman correlation   *d. multiple regression

51. Detective Johnson is interested in determining the extent to which formal education and parent's annual income can affect juvenile delinquency. He goes to a local high school and surveys the files of 1,000 current and former students who still live in the city. He determines the number of years of education completed by the mother, the father, and the student. He then contacts the parents and asks them to tell him the amount of their taxable income for the

preceding year. He then checks with the local juvenile detention center to determine the number of days that these students have spent in the center. What statistical technique should he use to find the relationship between delinquency on the one hand and education and income on the other?
a. linear-log analysis
b. factor analysis
*c. multiple regression
d. four-way mixed-regression ANOVA

52. Professor Taylor wants to determine if a student's class attendance and grade are related. He has the number of absences and overall class performance (out of 200 points) recorded for each student. How could he determine if the two variables are related?
*a. Pearson's r   c. multiple r
b. Spearman   d. log-linear analysis